PAPUA NEW GUINEA

Language

Grade 6

Teacher Resource Book

Susan Baing

253 Normanby Road, South Melbourne, Victoria 3205, Australia

Oxford University Press is a department of the University of Oxford. It furthers the University's objective of excellence in research, scholarship, and education by publishing worldwide in

Oxford New York

Auckland Cape Town Dar es Salaam Hong Kong Karachi Kuala Lumpur Madrid Melbourne Mexico City Nairobi New Delhi Shanghai Taipei Toronto

With offices in

Argentina Austria Brazil Chile Czech Republic France Greece Guatemala Hungary Italy Japan Poland Portugal Singapore South Korea Switzerland Thailand Turkey Ukraine Vietnam

First published 2005
Reprinted 2008 (twice), 2009, 2010, 2014

ISBN 978 0 19 555346 8

Designed and typeset by Lynn Twelftree
Printed in China by Golden Cup Printing Co. Ltd

Contents

Chapter 1 Overview

Introduction

This *Teacher Resource Book* is for teachers to use in conjunction with the *Language for Grade 6 Outcomes Edition* student textbook. It will help teachers implement the *Language Grade 6 Syllabus 2003 for Upper Primary Students* by providing teachers with:

- information for planning a school-based programme,
- a selection of teaching and learning strategies,
- a range of planning and assessment techniques, and
- ways to extend and develop content and student practice from the Student Book.

Key features of the Student Book

The Student Book is designed to help students achieve the outcomes given in the syllabus. Students will find models, examples and exercises to help them with the knowledge, skills, processes and attitudes as outlined in the syllabus. Speaking and listening, reading and writing skills are integrated. Students will find meaningful contexts to:

- use language effectively,
- increase their knowledge of language, and
- understand how language works.

The content of the Student Book:

- supports the *Language Grade 6 Syllabus 2003* by following the sequence of strands and sub-strands, while providing integration between strands and sub-strands,
- contains references to the *Upper Primary Language Syllabus* at the beginning of each chapter to show the clear relationship between the Student Book and the syllabus,
- provides four chapters for each of the strands of speaking and listening, reading, and writing,
- covers the sub-strands of production, skills and strategies, context and text, and critical literacy,
- provides topics and learning approaches that directly support the achievement of syllabus outcomes,
- includes a wide range of models, examples, exercises and activities that are student centred and provide a context for whole language learning,
- is presented in language appropriate for Grade 6 language learning,
- provides models and examples from Papua New Guinea that follow syllabus guidelines (*our way of life: cultural, multicultural, ethical, moral and showing values; and integrated human development: the right to healthy living, citizenship, sustainability)*,
- uses language that is gender sensitive and includes positive gender roles,
- uses illustrations to help students understand the text and to stimulate their imaginations, and
- allows students and teachers to supplement materials with other appropriate models and examples in English, Tok Pisin or vernacular languages.

Key features of the Teacher Resource Book

Each chapter contains the following sections:

- about this strand (the role of the strand in a language program),
- key words (major words that students and teachers will be using throughout the chapters),
- links to other main subjects,
- possible assessment tasks (suitable to assess skills learnt for the strand), and
- teacher information (added information for teachers in terms of specific content).

The Teacher Resource Book is designed to help teachers use the Student Book to successfully implement the *Upper Primary Language Syllabus* for Grade 6. Key topics are:

- learning and teaching strategies,
- planning suggestions and checklists,
- assessment procedures and checklists,
- assessment activities, and
- suggestions about how to further develop topics and integrate speaking and listening, reading and writing skills.

How to use the Teacher Resource Book

Learning outcomes

Outcomes-based education is used to identify and monitor progress in student learning. The emphasis is on what is actually learnt by each student rather than what is taught. An outcomes approach means identifying what students should achieve and focuses on ensuring that they achieve the identified outcome. Teachers focus on planning for student learning. Outcomes are written to measure the success of learning. The syllabus gives a series of outcomes agreed to be essential for all students to achieve.

Outcomes-based education

The language syllabus provides the knowledge, skills, attitudes and values that students should achieve in Grade 6. These are expressed as outcomes and indicators. These outcomes describe what the students should know, understand, value and be able to do. They are student centred and written in terms that mean they can be demonstrated, assessed and measured.

Each learning outcome is illustrated with a list of examples called *indicators*. These show the kind of things that students should be able to do, know and understand if they are achieving an outcome. Indicators can be used by teachers to monitor student progress within a level and to make judgements about the achievement of an outcome. Learning outcomes and indicators will:

- give teachers the flexibility to develop ideas presented in the Student Book to meet their students' needs,
- help teachers assess and report students' achievements in relation to the learning outcomes,
- allow student achievement of the outcomes to be described in consistent ways,
- help teachers monitor student learning, and
- describe what most students will know, and be able to do as a result of effective learning.

Developmental outcomes are also included. They aim to develop learners who are able to:

- reflect on and explore a variety of strategies to learn effectively,
- reflect on and explore a variety of strategies to communicate effectively,
- participate as responsible citizens in the life of local and national communities through the development of their language skills, and
- be culturally sensitive across a range of social contexts.

Learning and teaching strategies

The *Language Upper Primary Teachers Guide 2003* for Grade 6 states:
Language at Upper Primary is all about teaching students communication skills. To communicate effectively, students need to have a good understanding of a broad range of skills and processes. Language learning focuses on the development of the four key areas of language essential for effective communication: knowledge, skills, thinking processes and attitudes. These are explained in the *Language Teachers Guide* (see table, page 2).

When planning their learning and teaching strategies teachers need to take into account this extract from the National Curriculum Statement:
By Grade 6, English is the main language of instruction across the curriculum. Vernaculars, however, must continue to be encouraged and developed.

Teaching methods

The *Language Upper Primary Teachers Guide 2003* makes clear the key methods teachers should use:
Language is learnt when students are actively involved in genuine activities, in a supportive environment, where the teacher responds to students' needs and interests. Vital to this are the key ideas of interactive learning, whole language, and student-centred learning.

Interactive learning

Students learn language by:

- using it to discuss ideas,
- presenting their own knowledge and expertise on a topic, and
- listening to other students present their knowledge and expertise and working creatively with each other by talking to generate, refine and extend ideas.

An example is writing a role play about something that is important in the students' community (Chapter 1, Student Book).

Whole language

The whole language approach is used (refer to *Language Upper Primary Teachers Guide 2003*, page 3). The skills and processes needed to help students communicate and to respond to a wide range of real and literary experiences are emphasised. Students are encouraged to respond to a wide variety of texts. The Student Book provides a wide range of the genres for teachers to use and expand upon. Speaking and listening, reading and writing processes are not practised separately but as part of a whole language experience. For example, students could:

- begin with brainstorming a topic to be discussed,
- break into small groups to refine ideas,
- present group ideas to the class,
- write their own response to the class presentations,
- read other students' responses, and
- then discuss those responses.

Where possible, the process should be extended to the community, giving students opportunities to use language skills outside the classroom. Several activities in the Student Book show how this can be done.

In whole language, more emphasis is placed on the processes and skills than the finished product. Activities in the Student Book are broken into steps to guide students through the processes of language production. Language learning takes place through communication and the integration of skills and processes.

Student-centred learning

A student-centred approach is used. It focuses on learning as being the active construction of meaning by students, and teaching as the act of guiding and facilitating learning by:

- building on students' prior knowledge,

- using the community and its resources to give students the opportunity to use their language skills,
- providing opportunities for problem solving, decision making and taking action, and
- providing students with opportunities to reflect upon their own learning, knowledge, values, attitudes and language skills.

The role of teachers in student-centred learning is to provide a supportive environment in which students feel confident to produce language. Teachers can use material in the Student Book to create contexts which have meaning and purpose for the students. The teacher plans and models appropriate language forms in context, and observes and supports students as they go through a process, such as that described in the example above. The teacher will intervene in the process as appropriate to provide assistance and guidance. Much of the skills development takes place in cooperative pair or group situations where students consult each other, share ideas and learn from each other.

The *Language Upper Primary Teachers Guide 2003* lists points about the role of students (page 9). Student Book activities encourage students to develop these roles.

The *Guide* also provides details of key skills and strategies that can be used for each of the strands (pages 10–11) and both general and specific teaching and learning strategies which are appropriate for student-centred learning (pages 14–31). These can be combined with suggestions for learning given in the Student Book, and in the following chapters of this book.

Planning guidelines

The Student Book and the Teacher Resource Book do not provide planning for term, weekly or daily lessons. You need to:

- plan groups of lessons that use models and activities in the Student Book to enable learners to achieve the outcomes described in the syllabus, and
- fit each set of lessons into a short term work plan.

Use the table in the appendix as a checklist when planning lessons. Note that the assessment process is part of the planning process.

Assessment purposes

The purpose of assessment is to improve student learning by:

- collecting and analysing information about students' competencies,
- providing guidance, feedback and information about students' achievements and progress to students and parents, and
- helping to make decisions about improving programmes and classroom organisation.

The activities in the Student Book are designed to suit these purposes.

Assessment methods

Methods chosen should answer the questions teachers ask:

- What do I want to know?
- How will I find out?

The activities provided in the Student Book help teachers assess students' abilities to demonstrate the learning outcomes. The methods used should:

- enable teachers to closely monitor and understand students' progress,
- help teachers diagnose problem areas in both learning and teaching, and
- give learners helpful feedback after every assessment.

Teachers should refer to *Language Upper Primary Teachers Guide 2003* (pages 32–49) for both general and specific guidelines for assessment. Refer to the Appendices for some useful templates.

Speaking and listening

About this strand

Speaking and listening are together as a strand because it is usual for them to happen together. In the four chapters of this strand students will practise activities that lead to these skills:

- listening attentively to follow classroom instructions,
- listening to the teacher modelling speech,
- speaking and listening in discussions,
- speaking and listening in 'read aloud' and 'think aloud' sessions, and
- using language in different ways for different purposes, such as to instruct, or read a poem.

Many of the speaking and listening activities are integrated with reading and writing in both language and other subjects.

Knowledge of texts both written and oral is developed. Students learn how texts are structured in *narrative, recount, report, procedure, explanation* and *exposition.* Knowledge of the written text types is used to prepare for speaking various text types and listening to various text types.

Skills that are relevant to reading and writing underpin oral skills. Students develop the skills of *generic structure, cohesion, vocabulary, grammar, paragraphing and punctuation, word structure* and *procedural skills.* These are used in the specific speaking and listening skills of *interactive speaking and listening, oral presentation, grasping main points of talk, identifying particular details in talk, evaluating what is being said,* and *using and recognising non-verbal communication (gestures, facial expressions, body movements).*

Thinking processes that students will be involved in are relevant to each of the strands. They are *decision making, problem solving* and *strategic planning.*

Attitudes are also developed and the syllabus aims to develop students' enjoyment, confidence and independence as language users and learners. They will learn to *appreciate language, interact with others willingly with language* and *show that they have empathy and sensitivity towards others.*

Each chapter covers one of the outcomes. The outcomes can be used to measure students' achievements in creating and interpreting meaning from spoken language, developing spoken language and using spoken language correctly. The indicators are samples of the kind of activity you can plan to allow you to see if the outcome has been reached. The indicators given in the syllabus have been used as a basis for activities in the Student Book. You can plan other activities that can be used as indicators of the students' achievement of the outcome.

The activities and materials in the Student Book are not divided into lessons. You, as a teacher, will decide on the outcome to be taught and then select material for that outcome. Some material may be from different Language strands. The templates in the Appendix will help teachers use the Student Book and this book.

Key words

These are words that you as a teacher, and your students, will be using in the four chapters of the Speaking and Listening strand (in order of use in the Student Book). You will find an explanation of the words in Appendix 7, Glossary.

Student Book Chapter 1

speaking in different ways role play poetry imagine and pretend
important in the community read aloud story telling advertisements re-write

Student Book Chapter 2

question words information survey *(for more information see Teacher Information)*
polite reporting gestures conduct

Student Book Chapter 3

sense conversation instructions directions signal order formal

Student Book Chapter 4

context purpose audience bias stereotype findings

Speaking and listening

Links to other main subjects

Student Book Chapter 1

Throughout the twelve chapters of the Student Book, the first Learning Outcome to *communicate, for different purposes, locally relevant ideas to a variety of audiences* can be applied in most situations. Oral and written communication should follow this outcome.

'*Locally relevant ideas*' are part of the other curriculum areas, in particular Social Science, Making a Living and Personal Development.

'*To a variety of audiences*' emphasises the need to have close links with the community of which the school is part.

Role play Activity 1: Puppets can be used for role play in this activity and elsewhere as you feel appropriate.

Safety Activity 2: personal development.

Olympics Activity 3: current events, Social Science.

Family relationships Activities 4, 5: Social Science, Personal Development.

Advertising Activity 6: Social Science (consumer rights).

Student Book Chapter 2

Culture Activities 1–5: Social Science.

Cultural change Activities 6–9: Social Science.

Student Book Chapter 3

Culture Activities 2, 6, 8: Social Science.

Student Book Chapter 4

Interacting with other people Activity 3: Personal development.

Avoiding stereotype and bias Activity 4: Social Science, Personal Development.

Survey forms Activity 6: Social Science.

Possible assessment tasks

Teachers should follow the assessment guides and use the templates in the *Language Teachers Guide*, Upper Primary, 2003, pages 32 to 49. On page 49 the *Guide* states '*Language assessment in the classroom is not about comparing one student to another. It is about assessing the skills and knowledge students have mastered and those aspects they are having difficulties with so that more focussed guidance and attention can be given to individual students.*'

Some of the following activities are designed for students to measure their own achievements in terms of the outcomes for Speaking and Listening. Outcomes for Reading and Writing are also included. Students should be given chances to identify their strengths and weaknesses. Teachers can also use the tables as assessment guides. The tables below will give students an opportunity to do this. Following their responses they can adjust their learning. Any writing done should be added to the students' writing portfolios. Assessment for Speaking and Listening activities will take place mainly through observation.

You should observe and/or assess a student's ability to:

- select and talk about a range of topics,
- give or carry out instructions,
- talk with effect,
- respond to questions,
- summarise in their own understanding, presented information, and
- improvise to express and interpret information modelled.

(Page 19, Teachers Guide)

Activities throughout the Student Book can be used for assessment. Students can also self-assess and be assessed by their peers. A Peer Assessment form can be found in the *Teachers Guide* page 37.

Tests for Student Book Chapter One

In Chapter 1 students learn to talk in different ways about important things and how to listen to other people talking and acting.

1. Writing and performing role plays.

Write and perform a role play using the ideas in Chapter 1.

Ask the students to fill in this table. Students should tick off these things when they have finished the activities in the Student Book.

(*Note*: all such tables in this and the following chapters should be discussed with individual students as they are completing them. Give guidance about how to fill in the table. Stress the need for honest self-assessment.)

We talked about important things in our community so our group could decide what our role play would be about.	
We worked together to decide on the story and the characters for our role play.	
We wrote our role play.	
We practised our role play using different voices and faces.	
We performed our role play for the class.	
We listened to other groups doing their role plays.	
We talked about how ourselves and the other students talked in different ways.	
We put a copy of this role play and the other role plays we wrote into our writing portfolio.	

2. Writing and saying poems.

Poems in the Student Book can be used for this kind of assessment also.

Read this poem, then ask the students to write another poem of their own. Their poem should have feelings about someone or something that has gone or died.

Silent Drum *by Susan Baing*

I stare at the drum.
It is old and dusty in the corner of our house.
I think of my grandfather beating it for us to dance
  and sing.
Now he has gone
And it has no voice.

Ask the students to fill in this table. Students should tick off these things when they have finished the task.

We talked in a group about the feelings in the drum poem and how we could use our voices and faces to show the feelings in the poem.	
I wrote my own poem to tell about a sad feeling.	
I talked with a partner about my poem and how I would say it.	
I listened to my partner talk about their poem.	
I practised saying my poem, using my voice and face to show feelings.	
I said my poem to the class.	
I listened to the other students saying their poems and thought about the feelings in their poems.	
We talked about how ourselves and the other students talked in different ways.	
We put a copy of this poem and the other poems we wrote into our writing portfolio.	

3. Writing and telling stories.

Write a story about something important in the community. Use the ideas in Chapter 1.

Ask the students to fill in this table. Students should tick off these things when they have finished the task.

We talked in a group about important things in our community.	
We talked about what things we could write stories about.	
I wrote my story.	
I put in characters and feelings.	
I read my story to the class.	
I listened to the other students reading their stories.	
We talked about how ourselves and the other students talked in different ways.	
We put a copy of this story and the other stories we wrote into our writing portfolio.	

Tests for Student Book Chapter Two

In Chapter 2 students learn to talk to other people by asking questions. They learn how to talk and how to listen to others in a group, and how to use their face and body to help their listener understand them.

1. Using question patterns.

The teacher should provide a picture or use suggestions for Question 3. Ask the students to look at the picture and write a question starting with the words given.

1. When…
2. Where…
3. Why…
4. Who…
5. How…
6. What…
7. Which…
8. Do…
9. Are…
10. Should…

Tell the students to question a partner and listen to the answers. They should talk about the answers with each other. Here are some sample questions:

1. When did it rain?
2. Where is the octopus?
3. Why did the boy try to scare away the shark?
4. Who are the men in the fishing boat?
5. How do the boys catch fish?
6. What are the boys trying to catch?
7. Which way of fishing is better for the environment?
8. Do big fishing companies take too many fish?
9. Are sharks dangerous?
10. Should we have laws to protect fish in the sea?

2. Talking using our faces and bodies.

Tell the students to:

1. Use the questions and answers they have

Figure 1

used to make up an exciting story about the picture.

2. Write the story.
3. Read the story to a partner using their face and body to help the listener understand the story.
4. Put the story into their writing portfolio.

3. Having a discussion before doing a survey.
Use an environmental topic such as over-fishing. You should show this picture above from *The Pacific Series* (Oxford) *Using English, Pupils Book 2 Grade 6*, page 55.

The discussion should lead to this idea: if people are taking too many fish from the sea, soon the sea might not have enough fish for us to eat. The same thing is happening with other parts of our environment.

1. Talk in groups about something in your community environment that could be spoilt if people take away too much.
2. Ask the students to listen to the other members of the group.
3. Encourage the students to ask them questions when they don't understand or they want to know more.
4. Talk with the group about doing a survey to find out what other people in your community think about looking after the things in your community environment.
5. Ask them to plan what you will do in your survey and write the survey questions.

4. Do a survey and report on the survey.

1. Follow the way to do a survey and report on a survey in Chapter 2.
2. Put the written survey report and the survey report from Chapter 2 into their writing portfolios.
3. Get students to tell the class about the survey their group did. They should use their face and body to help the listeners understand.

5. Ask the students to fill in this table.

Students should tick off these things when they have finished the tasks.

I can ask questions using the ten sentence patterns.	
I can listen to answers to my questions.	
I can ask questions and listen to answers when I talk in a group.	
I can use my face and body to help my listener understand.	
I can listen and understand when someone uses their face and body when they are talking.	

Tests for Student Book Chapter Three

In Chapter 3 students learn about speaking at different times and in different places. They learn that it is important to use the right kind of words in conversations and when they are giving directions.

1. Having a conversation.

Use the picture in *The Pacific Series* (Oxford) *Using English, Pupils Book 2 Grade 6*, page 64.

Ask the students to:

1. Pretend they are one of the women in the garden, or the boy and girl mending the nets.
2. Take the part of one of the people and talk to the other person.
3. Listen to what their partner says and add to the conversation.

2. Giving instructions.

Now pretend one of the people is telling the other how to do something, such as how to mend the net or plant the vegetables.

1. Let the student choose which person they are—the gardener giving instructions or the net mender giving instructions.
2. Listen to the instructions the partner gives and ask questions if you do not understand.

Figure 2

Speaking and listening

3. Talking about how to go somewhere.

This is a role play for four students and their teacher. Use the map in *The Pacific Series* (Oxford) *Using English, Pupils Book 2 Grade 6*, page 68—include names on the map.

Figure 3

Here is a map of a village.
The teacher will pretend to be Mrs Hua, a new teacher at the school. She wants to know how to get to each of the student's houses from her house on the hill near the canoe beach. The students are called Kore, Pipi, Sisia and Heni.

1. Mrs Hua and the students have a conversation.
2. Each student will tell how to get to their own house.
3. The students must remember to talk the way they would talk to a teacher.
4. The students can talk to each other as well. Ask questions to make the directions clearer.

4. Ask the students to fill in this table.

Students should tick off these things when they have finished the tasks.

When we had a conversation, I took my turn and listened to what my friends said.	
In the conversation I made my sentences follow the words and ideas my friends used.	
When I gave instructions I put the steps in the right order.	
I helped my listener understand my directions by using signals.	
When I listened to the directions, I could understand them. If I did not understand, I asked questions to help me understand better.	
I gave clear directions for how Mrs Hua could get to my house.	
I used the right kind of language to talk to a teacher.	

Tests for Student Book Chapter Four

In Chapter 4 students use some different ways of talking, and talk about their own ideas. They learn that they should not have bias in their writing or talking, and they should not use stereotypes.

1. Talk in a group.

Remember what was learnt in Chapter 4. Use the picture in The Pacific Series (Oxford) *Using English*, Pupils Book 3 Grade 6, page 30.

The students should:

1. Say what they think has happened.
2. Say how it happened.
3. Say who they think caused that damage to the classroom.
4. Say what they think should be done.

Figure 4

2. Write a report on the event 'Classroom Destroyed'.

1. Think about what the group talked about.
2. The students should decide what their point of view is about people who spoil classrooms.
3. Make sure they do not use bias and stereotypes.

3. Give a speech to the group or the class that shows your point of view.

The students should:

1. Use all they have learnt about using face and body to help listeners understand.
2. Speak as if they are not talking to their friends, but to people they do not know.

4. Ask the students to fill in this table.

Students should tick off these things when they have finished the tasks.

I followed our class set of rules when we talked in a group.	
I did not use bias when we talked in a group, or in my report.	
I did not use stereotypes when we talked in a group, or in my report.	
I made my point of view clear in my speech.	
I put my report into my writing portfolio.	

Speaking and listening

Teacher information

In this section you will find information on the activities and background to some activities in the four chapters of the Speaking and Listening strand. The information is for you to use, if you wish, in helping you plan your lessons.

You will find the answers to Student Book Activities in Appendix 6.

Student Book Chapter 1 Talking in different ways about important things

6.1.1 Communicate, for different purposes, locally relevant ideas to a variety of audiences.

Sub-strand: Production—to provide opportunities for students to use language for real purposes. The emphasis for Chapter 1 is on use—students should be given every opportunity to talk and listen to real language.

Activity 1: Talk in different ways

Use the drawings to have a group discussion.

- What is happening in each picture?
- What could the children in each picture be saying? How would they say it?
- The students could act out what they think is being said.

Indicator: the students can role play a variety of characters vividly using puppets.

- Students will write their own role plays and teachers will note that they have different kinds of characters in them. Vividly means that the students should be deeply involved in the characters.

Activity 2: Imagine and describe

Introductory discussion:

- When have you ever pretended to be someone else? Who was it? What did you do? How did you speak?
- Organise students into groups of five. Allow ample time for practise. They should be able to read the parts fluently and with appropriate expression of voice and face.

Activity 3: Write your own play

Students can act or make puppets. Some students are comfortable with acting out, others may prefer to use an aid such as a puppet.

For you to try: every community will have issues which are discussed. The role play should be about locally relevant ideas—but don't forget humour.

Step 1: sample answers

1. I think we should make our role play about (*students add a locally relevant idea*).
2. I think malnutrition is a problem in our community. I think our role play should be about telling mothers what foods are good for babies to eat.
3. It is important in our community to know about (*students add a locally relevant idea*).
4. We have a disabled child in our school. I think our role play should be about how we can help a child who is blind.

Step 2

This can be done in a pyramid method:

1. Begin with students writing own ideas.
2. Students then share with a partner.
3. Two partners join as a group.
4. The group reports to the class.
5. Students can all do the same role play or they can do as many different role plays as you wish.

➢ After the ideas have been gathered, and a decision made about the topic for the role play(s), form groups and begin the discussion on character and plot.

Step 3: characters

➢ The number of characters should be limited. Group size will determine the number. Characters can be people or animals.

➢ Check on gender equity and suggest female characters if they are lacking.

➢ Characters should be believable.

➢ Characters should be like people they know so that the students can act the parts.

➢ Look for portrayal of positive roles.

Step 4

➢ Group decisions should be made based on equal participation.

➢ Do not allow students to go on until they have a rough plan that all in the group have agreed to.

Step 5

➢ Students could be allocated the characters they are to play at this point and begin to plan what they will say in their character.

➢ The group should work progressively through the play, with full discussion before character speeches are accepted.

➢ The group should aim for each character to be fairly equal in the amount they speak.

Step 6

➢ Group members can take turns to record carefully what the speeches are.

➢ Explain about stage directions: these are directions to the characters. They can tell the characters how to speak, or how to move, or where to go.

Step 7

➢ Allow ample time for students to become fluent. Encourage appropriate emotions and facial expressions.

➢ The role play should be added to the writing portfolio.

Indicator: the students can recite their own poems meaningfully, displaying a range of images and emotions.

➢ To recite is to say aloud, often without referring to a written text.

Activity 4: Read aloud

➢ 'Children run' is a simple poem. It is a sample of the kind of 'own' poems the students could write.

➢ Refer to Reading and Writing outcomes.

Using voice: The activities are designed to extend the range of emotions the students are able to portray.

➢ Allow time for practise and encourage 'meaningful' recitation.

For you to try: students write their own poems following the sample poem, or any type of poem you wish. The poem should be added to the writing portfolio.

Indicator: the students can retell oral stories of some complexity in an interesting manner, individually or in groups.

➢ To retell means to take a story already written and tell it in a different way. 'Of some complexity' means that the story should have some development of plot and character and some twists and turns.

Activity 5: Telling stories in an interesting way

A sample story is given. Students can use the sample to practise reading. If the story seems too long, divide up the story and students can work together in groups on different sections.

- Read the story to a partner.
- Students should read the story to themselves first, making note of where to pause, and how to show the meaning of the story.

Make the story sound interesting. Teacher should demonstrate this to the students.

Facial expression: Teacher should show examples.

For you to try:

Step 1

- This should be an individual choice.
- The story should be of a reasonable length.
- Refer back to the Learning Outcome 'locally relevant ideas'.

Step 2

- Students should be asked to identify and list the feelings they will need to show when reading the story.

Step 3

- Refer to Activity 3 above about using different facial expressions.

Step 4

- Demonstrate words, emotions and facial expressions. There are other ways to make the reading of the story interesting.

Step 5

- Allow students ample time to practise.
- You may want them to write the story down, or they could rely on written notes. If written, the story should be added to the writing portfolio.

Step 6

- Students can perform for the whole class if they are confident enough.
- They could also perform for parents, teachers or other classes. (Refer to *Learning Outcome 'to a variety of audiences'.*)

Indicator: the students can perform a range of imaginative texts, including narratives, poetry, scripts and advertisements.

Advertising

- Teachers to use whatever advertising material is available to them—newspapers, radio, television, or billboards.
- Find out what students know about the purpose of advertising. What advertisements are they familiar with?

Activity 6: Speaking a written advertisement

A sample advertisement is given. Students should practise, then perform.

- Explain how an advertisement is set out, and explain any difficult words (please note that the original advertisements had some very hard words, and these have been changed for the text book).
- Teacher can model some actions, for example actions to make the advertisement stronger such as flexing muscles.

Activity 7: Re-write an advertisement

- Groups discuss the advertisement for Arrow Beef biscuits.
- There are two children in the advertisement. Students should note the lines '*Liklik prais oltaim!*' and '*Always hits the spot!*' Point out the exclamation marks at the end of the sentences and explain how to say the lines.
- The words in the advertisement are like a joke. '*Always hits the spot*' is talking about the arrows in the name *Arrow Beef* and about how good they are.
- *This will need to be discussed.* The advertisement makes a pun or joke with words. The biscuits name and illustration is Arrow. A good aim can make the arrow hit the bullseye or 'spot'. To hit the spot is an idiom in English. It means to be very good, just the right thing (to eat).

- Give examples of words that can be used—delicious, tasty. 'Always' makes it stronger.
- Actions for the advertisement should be appropriate, for example shooting an arrow.

Activity 8: Write a new advertisement

Go through the steps with the students. Talk about the kind of words the advertisement would need—persuasive words.

Do some more talking. These materials in the Student Book can be used at any time.

Students should use all the techniques of meaningful reading they have learnt.

The stories, plays or poems can be used as writing models.

The stories and poems can be made into role plays.

Poems can be acted out with movements.

For plays, begin with discussion of movement about the 'set' and expression of character.

Student Book Chapter 2
Talking to other people: asking questions

6.1.2 Apply a range of speaking and listening skills on both familiar and introduced topics in spontaneous and structured activities.

Sub-strand: Skills and Strategies acknowledging the importance of skills and strategies necessary to effectively communicate.

Indicator: students can ask relevant questions using who, what, why, when, how and where.

Activity 1: Why do we ask questions?

There should be group discussions of the role of questions in oral communication. The groups should report to class.

Activity 2: Answering questions

Students should break into pairs and ask questions and listen to answers. Stress to students that they must listen actively to the answers as they will use the material they hear to write a paragraph about their partner. They then use the information gained to tell the group about their partner.

Activity 3: Question words

1. Explain the work of question words in a sentence—how they act as a signal to tell us that a question is coming.
   Individual exercise—tell a partner their answers. See if the partner agrees.
2. Identify each type of question word. Students should be able to explain why that question word was used in the sentence.
3. Questions should be spoken correctly: the tone of the speaker's voice should rise slightly towards the end of the sentence.

Activity 4: Writing questions

1. Teacher to do an example.
2. Groups discuss the picture and the text. Decide what kind of questions could be used. Individuals write their own questions and then, with a partner, ask the questions and listen to the answers.

Activity 5: Questions about culture

Individual followed by pair work. Teachers can use any further pictures available if more practice is needed.

For you to try: give students a topic to write their own questions about. The topic should be school or community based and be something that the other students can provide answers for.

Indicator: the students can create and conduct an oral survey in the local community (6.1.1).

➢ This indicator is included in Chapter 2 because of the need for questioning skills to be taught first.

Activity 6: Ideas about asking questions in surveys

In pairs read the two role plays. Students can perform for the class.

1. Discuss the role plays in groups to answer the questions. Teacher points out oral clues showing familiarity, for example *Uncle*, which will use informal questions form; and oral clues showing formal address, which will use the formal question form.

Answers: first, students should ask if it is a good time to ask the questions; the students should say why they are asking the questions; they should say why the survey is being done; the questions need to be written down; the answers need to be written down.

A note on questions for surveys and setting out of survey response sheet.

Students will act in groups of four. All four students will interview the same people, one after another. This will require you to do some research and make sure that there are people willing to be interviewed.

Topics 1, 2 and 3 require factual answers; Topic 4 is asking for opinion. This will affect the way the questions are written and asked.

Topic 1: There are three parts to the topic. Students should write one question for each part. Students will ask open-ended questions for each part. These are questions that need to be answered by a sentence reply, not yes/no. They should draw up a table of three columns for their answers.

Topic 2: There are three parts to the topic. Students should write one question for each part. Some questions can be to get a yes/no answer, for example, *Do you make...any more? Yes/No*. They will need to cooperate with the student who is asking the questions for the first topic so that the replies carry on.

Topic 3: There are two parts to the topic. The questions and interviewing will follow on from Topics 1 and 2. The questions will be open-ended.

Topic 4: Some questions can be to get a yes/no answer, for example, *Do you think it is bad to change our culture? Yes/No*. This should be followed up with an open-ended question to get reasons why yes or no was given as an answer. The questions will follow on from previous question topics.

For you to try: this is a practise run before students conduct their own survey. Role play should be part of the practice. Go through the steps to make sure students know what to do.

➢ The topic should fit in with the outcome 'locally relevant ideas'.

➢ Use group knowledge to answer some initial questions (activate knowledge), then write questions which are outside the group's knowledge (known to unknown).

➢ Could library research be part of the survey? This will depend on your available sources.

Activity 7: Find out how your culture has changed

Students do the survey as a group of four. The given focus is cultural change; however, teachers can use another topic relevant to their community. Each student (or pair of students) will focus on one of the four ideas. They will work individually or as pairs to go through the five steps.

Indicator: the students can use appropriate facial expressions, gestures, intonation for communicating ideas and feelings.

➢ Students will show that they can fit the words they are saying with the expression on their face and the movements of their body.

Activity 8: Making your voice interesting

Further practice on extending oral skills.

Activity 9: Using gestures

Discuss the illustrations. Students complete the sentences: 2 agreement; 3 disagreement; 9 be quiet; 10 hello, I see you.

- Get the students to demonstrate the gestures to each other.
- What other gestures do they know—are their any gestures that are traditional, cultural or specific to their community?

Indicators: students can engage in group discussion logically to solve a problem; listen to show respect for the contribution of another student in the group; demonstrate ways to engage an audience and keep its attention.

- These skills can be practised at group level to begin with and can be extended to the class.

For you to try: students work individually or in pairs, following steps in Activity 7. Stress that recording answers properly is needed to write up the report.

- Group discussion should cover such problems as in which order to present the information, methods of presenting information, roles of various group members.
- Observe that students are achieving the outcome indicators.
- The activity should end with oral presentation of reports.

A note on report writing

Report writing is a specialised skill. However, the basics can be learnt now.

Refer to *English for Melanesia*, Book 2 for a sample report.

Grade 6 students can understand that there are parts to a report.

Introduction: this gives the reason for the report, for example 'We wrote this report because we are worried about the way our traditional skills are being lost.'

Methods: this part of the report explains how the students got the information, for example 'We asked the older people in the community for their ideas and about what they think.'

Findings: Write some sentences about what they found out, for example ' We found that many old people have not taught anyone how to make…'

Conclusion: What they think about what they have found out, for example 'We think that some of our traditional skills will be lost.'

Recommendations: What the students think can be done, for example 'We think our older people should come to school to show us how to make traditional things.'

- Point out that students can use numbers in their report for different paragraphs. For example, as there are four questions to be asked there could be four numbered paragraphs in the findings section. The report should be added to the writing portfolio.

Student Book Chapter 3 Speaking differently at different times and places

6.1.3 Listen to and identify how spoken language is adapted to its context.

Sub-strand: Context and Text refers to the importance of learning and using language in different situations and the fact that how we communicate influences the kind of text we use.

Indicators: the students can select and use descriptive language appropriate to the context; demonstrate an ability to turn-take in conversations.

Activity 1: Making sense

- Stress the importance of making sense when communicating.
- Use the picture for students to generate more sentences about the picture. In pairs say sentences which make 'sense' or 'non-sense'. Partners to comment on sense or nonsense.

Activity 2: Role play

Students role play using the picture to generate a character. They should talk in character.

Activity 3: Making conversation

- Students work in pairs. Practise and perform, using skills of using voice learnt so far.
- Discuss the three questions in pairs. Students should tell their ideas about the three questions to another pair.
- Island Life 2: compare the two conversations. In the second conversation, the conversers are not listening to responses so the conversation does not make sense. Stress the need for active listening in conversation so that you can respond sensibly.

Activity 4: A muddled conversation

Students to work in pairs to discuss the two options for each part of the conversations. They should pick out the reply which is the result of active listening and correctly responding. When they have decided, they should read the whole conversation aloud, using appropriate voice and gesture.

Activity 5: Writing a conversation

Students to work in pairs. Students will first work individually—this shows them that you need two people to make a conversation, and that a conversation is built up of responses, not individual comments. Students should negotiate to arrive at a conversation which makes sense.

Indicators: students can show knowledge of signalling language to sequence events; use appropriate specialised features in a variety or oral texts; show a knowledge of language structures, for example accurately giving directions in sequence.

Teachers should refer to Chapter 9.

Activity 6: Questions about the conversation about making kambang

- Students read, then role play the conversation 'Kambang'.
- Without looking back at the conversation, work in pairs to attempt to put the sentences in order.
- Teacher discusses signals with students, demonstrating the work of each signal used in the 'Kambang' conversation. Talk about the order the signals were used in.

Activity 7: Changing a conversation

Students to practise adapting conversation and instruction giving for context of audience. They should speak simply and explain more about some of the instructions.

Activity 8: Muddled instructions

Order is very important in instructions—when you are giving instructions it is confusing to go back and say—*Oh, I forgot to tell you to do this first.* This is not generally a problem in written instructions.

- Work individually to put the sentences in order.
- Students compare answers with a partner, and then with that partner turn the text into a conversation.
- Read the conversation to a group and discuss.

Activity 9: Writing instructions

- Students begin with a discussion of each step in the picture. The steps should be listed before the conversations are attempted.
- The conversations should be written down. They are on two different levels (context of audience).
- Finished conversations can be performed for the class.

Activity 10: Order and signals

- In pairs students read the conversation 'The way to the bank'. Without looking back at the directions, attempt to put them in the right order. Students can look back at the map but not the text.
- Discuss the fact that only one signal has been used 'next'. Could more be used? Where would the students put them?

Activity 11: Putting directions in the right order

- Students use the same map as for Activity 10.
- Students should use similar signals to those suggested for Activity 10.
- When the sentences are in correct order, students work in pairs to turn the text into conversation.
- Perform the conversation.

Activity 12: Telling how to go somewhere

- Students work in pairs. After discussion of the map, cooperate to write the three conversations (formal, between equals, simpler for an elementary student).
- Check that students are using signals.

For you to try: extension work on conversation making and performing.

Student Book Chapter 4
How well do you listen and talk?

6.1.4 Respond to their own speaking and listening, while considering their own experiences and those of the community.

Sub-strand: Critical Literacy acknowledges that language learners and users need to think beyond content and recognise and evaluate the beliefs that influence texts.

Indicator: students can use and compare different types of oral communication.

Activity 1: Matching pictures and stories

- In pairs students read the six conversations, then perform them for a group of 12 students.
- They should indicate which picture their conversation is about.
- Group discussion should help students understand context for oral communication—how we use different ways of speaking depending on the context and how to realise what these differences are.

Activity 2: Your own conversation

- Groups of five students take one of the topics (teacher should provide further locally relevant topics) and use language appropriate to the topic.
- They should then perform the conversation for another group of five students who should be able to guess the topic from the vocabulary used and the manner of speaking.

Indicator: the students can explain and give examples of positive statements and negative statements that will not offend the listener.

- Students will hold different ideas and opinions about topics. They need to know what is acceptable in terms of making a different point of view clear without offending the listener.

Activity 3: Talking when you do not agree

- Discuss 'Being polite'. Students in groups discuss the kind of conversations they have had recently. Did they disagree with someone?
- Read conversations in pairs and compare them.
- Answer the questions.

Activity 4: Talking about bias and stereotype

- Read the sentences and passages aloud.
- Discuss bias and stereotypes—give any examples from your own community.
- Group work: get the students to answer the questions for each sentence and passage.
- They should write their own examples of sentences or passages with stereotype and bias and show them to the group. Discuss the students own sentences and passages.

Indicator: students can compose and perform oral texts that present a particular point of view.

Teachers should refer to Chapters 9 and 12.

Activity 5: Group talking

- Students read the comment in pairs. Each pair gets their ideas ready for presentation to the group.
- After the group discusses the letter they should analyse their own and other students' participation in the conversation.
- The list of rules should be discussed in the group, then written down.
- Groups share their list of rules with the class.
- Consensus on the rules should come from classroom discussion. The rules should be added to the writing portfolio.
- Teacher prepares the rules on a poster for future reference.

Activity 6: Working on a group survey and report

Use previous methods outlined to get ready for the survey. Revise question form and oral question asking.

Steps 1 and 2

- The topic should fit in with the outcome 'locally relevant ideas'.
- Make sure the topic chosen is important to the community and within the scope of the students' abilities.
- Students use proposal forms in Social Science. Assist students to copy forms accurately and fill them in meaningfully.
- Revise 'purpose'.
- Go over the sample. Discuss each point on the form.

Steps 3 to 6

- Students use their 'conversation and discussion' rules for group consensus.
- Reading and writing skills are an important part of this activity.
- The survey form should be checked by the teacher before it is used by the students.
- Written report writing can be a group effort, with students doing parts of the report.
- The written report is the basis for the oral presentation. The oral presentation should be a group effort with different students presenting sections of the report. Remind students that they can use graphs, tables or other visual material.
- Arrange for a wider audience (Learning Outcome 6.1.1).

Indicators: students can identify bias and stereotypes within a range of oral texts; role play alternative responses to an issue of local significance.

Activity 7: Role play

Role play can be used in preparation for presentation to a wider audience. The role play should be added to the writing portfolio.

Extension role play: students to act as the audience for the report—and respond negatively or positively. Role play the discussion that would follow.

Reading

About this strand

When teaching reading skills teachers need to keep in mind the language principles stated in the *Language Teachers Guide.*

In the four chapters of this strand students will practise activities that lead to these understandings:

- that reading is for enjoyment, for locating information and for making meaning,
- that good readers know what processes they use when they are reading,
- that good readers know how to make predictions. They base this on what they know about words, about the correct use of words and correct sentences, how certain kinds of writing are structured, and what they know about the topic before they start reading,
- that good readers know that there are several skills they can use to help them find and remember the meaning of what they are reading, and
- that good readers think about what they have read. They make judgements about what they have read. They base these judgements on their own values and on their own experiences of the world.

(Based on *Language Teachers Guide*, page 6.)

The areas of knowledge, skills, thinking and attitudes are developed in the Student Book.

1. Students' knowledge of written texts is developed. Students learn through reading how texts are structured in *narrative, recount, report, procedure, explanation* and *exposition.*
2. Various skills are learnt to develop students' competencies in learning and using language in a broad range of contexts: *generic structure, cohesion, vocabulary, grammar, paragraphing and punctuation, word structure* and *procedural skills.*
3. Thinking processes are those in which students' ideas, feelings and mental images are accessed, rearranged and presented. The processes of *decision making, problem solving* and *strategic planning* are used in reading.

Attitudes are also developed and the syllabus aims to develop students' enjoyment, confidence and independence as language users and learners. They will learn to *appreciate language, interact with others willingly with language* and *show that they have empathy and sensitivity towards others.*

Each chapter covers one of the outcomes. The outcomes can be used to measure students' achievements in creating and interpreting meaning from written language. The indicators are samples of the kind of activity you can plan to allow you to see if the outcome has been reached. The indicators given in the syllabus have been used as a basis for activities in the Student Book. Many of the reading activities in the Student Book are integrated with speaking and listening and writing in both Language and other subjects. You can plan other activities that can be used as indicators of the students' achievement of the outcome.

The activities and materials in the Student Book are not divided into lessons. You, as a teacher, will decide on the outcome to be taught and then select material for that outcome. Some material may be from different Language strands. The templates in the Appendix will help teachers use the Student Book and this book.

Key words

These are words that you as a teacher, and your students, will be using in the four chapters of the Reading strand (in order of use in the Student Book). You will find an explanation of the words in Appendix 7, Glossary.

Student Book Chapter 5

real world imaginary world events characters title information orientation complication resolution time words/signals narrative sequence chronological sequence cartoons cartoon balloons/bubbles shadow puppet process

Student Book Chapter 6

punctuation word attack skills context (for word attack skills) rhythm pattern repeated sound unit/syllable verse key word phrase summary heading topic sentence headline predicting

Student Book Chapter 7

plot theme setting ending fact/factual opinion action conflict compare

Student Book Chapter 8

genre personal preference dilemma alternatives justify

Links to other main subjects

Student Book Chapter 5

Gender roles, village activities Activity 1: Social Science

Ethical issues, Activity 3: Personal Development.

Shadow puppets, Activity 11: Art.

Student Book Chapter 6

Traditional songs and legends, Social Science, our culture.

Storing food, Personal Development.

Student Book Chapter 7

Pre-history/archaeology, Social Science.

Conservation (Jacob), Social Science

Student Book Chapter 8

Research skills, *Indicator: Look up the same reference in two non-fiction source texts and compare the helpfulness and presentation of the information given.*

This is part of the Social Science Process.

Conservation, Endangered species, cultural change, Social Science.

Family values, family roles, Personal Development.

Possible assessment tasks

The following activities are designed for students to measure their own achievements in terms of the Outcomes for Reading. Outcomes for Speaking and Listening and Writing are also included.

Teachers should follow the assessment guides and use the templates in the *Language Teachers Guide*, Upper Primary 2003, pages 32 to 49.

Some of the following activities are designed for students to measure their own achievements in terms of the outcomes for Reading. Teachers can also use the tables as assessment guides. Activities throughout the Student Book can be used for assessment.

Assessment for Reading activities will take place mainly through observation of students at work—their reading behaviours and strategies used.

Observations take place before, during and after reading. Assessment takes place during:

- silent reading,
- small group interaction,
- shared reading, and
- discussion.

Students can also be assessed through their written responses. Reading logs and reading journals should be kept.

Tests for Student Book Chapter Five

In Chapter 5 students read about the real world and about the imaginary world. They learn how a story is put together by the writer. They learn how to follow written instructions.

Students should read this story. They will do five things with the story.

A few years ago my dad bought a car. He was very proud of the car. It was not a new car, but an old car he bought from another man. My mother called it Ros Kar because it had a lot of rust on it. The car was painted different colours. The roof was red, the doors blue and the back was brown. But we loved that car. We went everywhere in it.

One day we set off to visit our grandmother. She lived in a village near the town where my father worked as a policeman. It was not very far but there were a lot of hills. At first we went along the road without any problems. Then we came to the first hill. The car was going well up the hill. But suddenly my mother noticed some smoke coming from the floor near her feet. Next she felt her feet getting hot.

'Stop the car!' she called out to my father and he quickly pulled to the side of the road. And then we all climbed out as quickly as we could.

My father ran around to the passenger side. He pulled up the rubber mat on the floor. He could see that there was a rusted hole in the floor and some paper had been put over the hole. Some of the paper had fallen on to the hot exhaust pipe and caught fire. My sister saw what had happened and she quickly poured her bottle of water on the fire. The fire went out. After the excitement we all sat down on the side of the road to rest. At last we all felt quiet enough to get back in the car again. And we set off once more down the road.

1. Make a plan of the story.

1. Give the story a title.
2. Draw up a plan of the story like Chapter 5.
3. Fill in the parts of the plan.

2. Draw a time line to show the order of the events in the story.

1. Use the list of events in the story that were put on the story plan.
2. Put the events on a time line from the start of the story to the end.

Answers:

- The car was bought a few years ago.
- One day (a few years later) we went for a drive.
- The journey went well.
- We came to some hills and the car caught fire.
- The fire was put out.
- The journey continued.

Reading

3. Make a list of the time words and other words that help to understand when things happened in the story.

Answers: a few years ago, one day, at first, then, suddenly, next, and then, after, at last, once more.

4. Draw a cartoon of the story.

Students can be asked to draw the carton for the whole story, or part of the story.

5. The students should write some instructions that would help another student draw a time line from a real or imaginary story.

Sample of what the students might write:

First you must read the story carefully.

Then read the story again to see the order that things happen in the story. You must remember that sometimes the person who writes the story can put the things that happen in a different order.

Make a list of the things that happen in the real order of time (this may be different from the order they are written in the story).

Draw a line on your page. The line must be long enough for you to write all the events. (Sometimes you need to practise first.)

Put the events in order along the line.

Leave more space when a long time happens and put events close together when they happen in a short time.

Give your time line a title.

6. Ask the students to fill in this table.

Students should tick off these things when they do them:

I can find the plan of a story.	
I can see how time is used in a story.	
I can find time words in a story and I know how they help me understand a story.	
I can write a set of instructions.	

Reading

Tests for Student Book Chapter Six

In Chapter 6 students learn some ways to be a better reader.

1. Patterns in sound. Read this poem:

Tapura Spring
translated by Karipe Pitzz, Huli

Today is dry
Tomorrow is cloudy
Yesterday a thunderstorm
All come and go
Tapura is timeless

Fruit ripen and rot
Pitpit flowers and dies
Man arrives today
He is gone tomorrow
Tapura is timeless.

(*Using English,* Pupils Book 1, Grade 6, page 78)

1. Find the sound patterns in this poem. Use the way of doing this that was explained in Chapter 6.
2. Ask the students to plan how they would use this to help them read the poem aloud.
3. If students find any new words, tell them to use the way they learnt in Chapter 6 to help them say the words.
4. Students should practise reading the poem aloud then read it to the group.

Answers:

Sound patterns:
Line 1 – 4 sounds
Line 2 – 6 sounds
Line 3 – 7 sounds
Line 4 – 4 sounds
Line 5 – 6 sounds
Line 6 – 5 sounds
Line 7 – 6 sounds
Line 8 – 5 sounds
Line 9 – 6 sounds
Line 10 – 6 sounds

2. Finding key words and phrases.

Work in groups to find key words and phrases in this story. Students should take turns to say what they think are the key words and phrases, and then work individually to write a summary.

> The cyclone arrived at last in our village. We had heard warnings about it on the radio. The wind was blowing at sixty or seventy kilometres an hour. Huge waves were pounding on the beach. Our house began to shudder and the wood began to creak and groan. The roof lifted as if it would fly away, but didn't because of the strong vines my father had used. Rain beat against the walls and came in through the cracks and through the windows. Our family sat close together and shivered. We thought that the house would be destroyed. We waited for the storm to pass. After a few hours the wind slowed down. We all went outside to see what damage had been done.

Sample answers: cyclone, warnings, radio, strong winds, waves pounding, roof lifted, rain came in, storm slowed, see damage.

3. Predict a story from headings.

1. Talk about the title and the headings below in a group. Students should take turns to say what they think will follow each heading in the story.
2. Now ask students to work individually to write the story, following the headings.

Title: Girls are marine experts
(*The National*, 18/02/04)
Two girls work with World Wildlife Fund
Their main activities
How they became marine experts
Their beliefs

4. Punctuation

Write a short story. Use as many kinds of punctuation as possible. Remember to put some talking (dialogue) in the story.

5. Ask the students to fill in this table.

Students should tick off these things when they have finished the tasks:

I can use what I know about words patterns to help me read a poem aloud and understand it better.	
I can talk in a group and give my ideas as well as listen to other students' ideas.	
I can pick out key words and phrases in a story.	
I can use key words and phrases to make a summary.	
I can predict what will happen from headings in a story.	
I can understand how punctuation works in a story.	

Tests for Student Book Chapter Seven

In Chapter 7 students learn some ways of knowing if they were reading facts or imaginary stories.

1. Work in a group.

1. Write down a list of ways to tell if a story is an imaginary story or a factual story.
2. Students should read their list to the group.
3. Talk about the ideas that the group gives.

2. Fact or opinion

Here are some sentences about the story in Chapter 5 *The Scary Watermelon.*

Get the students to decide if the sentence you read is a fact or opinion and put F or O in the space.

Singu was proud of his watermelons.	
Singu was the best gardener in the village.	
Singu should have been more generous to the children.	
Singu decided to scare the children.	
Singu made a plan of what to do.	
Singu's plan was very clever.	
The boys went towards the biggest watermelon.	
The boys will not come back to the garden again.	

Answers: F, O, O, F, F, O, F, O.

Reading

3. A new ending for a story.

1. The students should write a new ending for the story *The Scary Watermelon.*
2. Start with this sentence from the story: *'That melon! That melon!' shouted one boy. 'It's got eyes and a mouth!'*
3. Each should read the new ending to the group.

4. Ask the students to fill in this table.

Students should tick off these things when they have finished the tasks:

I know when a story is fact or imagination.	
I know the kinds of things that imaginary stories have.	
I know the kinds of things that factual stories have.	
I know the difference between fact and opinion.	
I can write another ending to a story.	

Tests for Student Book Chapter Eight

In Chapter 8 students think about which stories and poems they liked. They think about why they like some stories and poems but not others. They think about stories that give us some good ideas about the communities we live in.

Ask the students to fill in this table. Students should tick off these things when they have finished the activities in the Student Book.

I can think about ideas in factual stories about communities and their life.	
I can think about ideas in imaginary stories about communities and their life.	
I can decide which stories or poems I like or don't like.	
I can tell why I like or don't like a story or poem.	

Ask the students to fill in this table.

Students should tick off these things when they have finished the activities in the Student Book.

I can think about what the characters in the stories and poems say and do and decide if I agree with their actions.	
I can think about other ways the characters could act.	
I can think about what might happen after the end of the story or poem.	
I can think of other ways the story or poem could end.	
I can think about things that are important to the characters and communities in the stories and poems and decide what would be a solution to a problem.	
I know places to go to get information that will help me make decisions about problems like the ones in the stories and poems	

Teacher information

In this section you will find information on the activities and background to some activities in the four chapters of the Reading strand. The information is for you to use, if you wish, in helping you plan your lessons.

There are some key skills and processes that teachers need to use for teaching reading using the Student Book. These key skills and processes apply to any reading task you give your students.

Reading effectively means using a three stage process. Each time a reading task is approached, decide how you can best use these three stages:

1. Before reading students should:

- look,
- talk,
- share their ideas in a pair or group situation, and
- make predictions about any text and any diagrams, graphs or pictures that accompany the text.

2. During reading students should:

- join in the reading,
- read on further in the text or read back in the text,

- use pictures that accompany the text to help them interpret the text,
- make mental pictures of their own,
- attempt to clarify what they are reading,
- make use of cues from the meaning of words, the sounds of letters and letter groups and grammatical structures of sentences, and
- attempt to sound out and discover the meaning of unknown words.

3. After reading students should:

- talk about what they have read,
- think about the content, ideas and issues in what they have read,
- share their thoughts with other students in a pair or group situation,
- compare their own thoughts with other students and justify their ideas,
- practise substituting words or ideas or writing new endings to stories,
- go beyond the text they have read and make comments, and
- analyse the content.

The *Language Teachers Guide* pages 19 to 27 provides reading strategies for the teacher to use in teaching reading. These can be applied to the activities in the Student Book.

You will find the answers to Student Book Activities in Appendix 6.

Student Book Chapter 5
Reading about the real world; reading about the imaginary world

6.2.1 Read and respond to a range of texts about real and imaginary worlds.

Sub-strand: Production—to provide opportunities for students to use language for real purposes.

Indicator: students can map out the main stages of a story in order to explore narrative order.

Narrative order is the order of events or the plot in a story.

Activity 1: Questions about 'A Feast in the Village'

Begin the activity with a prediction exercise, using the title (a feast is happening; it is in the village) and the picture.

Day Dreams: students will use this activity to add signals for narrative order in Activity 5.

Activity 2: Questions about 'Day Dreams'

- Predictions from title (day dreams are when your mind drifts off, and even though you are awake, it is like you are dreaming). Hannah is the character (Who?). Hannah is actually in the classroom.
- Questions 4, 5 and 6 concern narrative order.
- *The Scary Watermelon*: begin with a prediction exercise.
- Use the right hand column to show how the story can be mapped out.

Activity 3: Plan of the story

Explain new vocabulary and the idea of mapping the parts of stories.

Activity 4: Time words in 'The Scary Watermelon'

Examples of time words: one afternoon, then…

Activity 5: Time signals in 'Day Dreams'

Discuss the meanings of the time words.

Activity 6: Adding time signals to 'A Feast in the Village'

Work in pairs to decide where time words are needed and what time words can be put in, for example—*That morning the village looked…*

There will be variations in student response. This can be discussed in groups.

Indicator: the students can draw a time line to show how time passes in a story and identify the vocabulary used to show the passing of time.

➢ Time in a story does not always follow chronological time. The story can begin in the middle of an event and then go back in time to show how that event developed. As students learn the vocabulary that writers use to show time, they will understand the sequence of events.

Activity 7 and Activity 8: Questions and time signals in 'Cat Food'

➢ Begin with a prediction exercise.

➢ The story starts on Thursday afternoon and finishes the next morning. The story goes in order, apart from sentences 2 and 3, which happen earlier in the day.

Indicator: the students can role play accurately a scene from a story previously read.

Activity 9: Role play of a story

Group students and give different stories for them to role play. The role play should be added to the writing portfolio.

Indicator: produce a short cartoon sequence with dialogue from a written story.

Activity 10: Making a cartoon

➢ Students should look at as many cartoons as you can provide—newspapers are a good source.

➢ Show students the relationship between the drawings and the speech balloons/bubbles. Students can role play the cartoon in the Student Book, and their own cartoon. The cartoon should be added to the writing portfolio.

Indicator: students can identify and note features of an instructional text such as a recipe, game, direction or an experiment.

➢ Instructional texts follow a pattern. Students need to recognise the features of that pattern.

Activity 11: Understanding the process

➢ Note layout of instructions—two parts *things needed* and *steps taken.*

➢ Discuss the role of the diagram.

➢ Provide more examples for students to answer similar questions about.

➢ Students can follow the instructions and make shadow puppets for role plays. Another way of showing shadow puppets is to hang a white sheet with a light source behind it. Puppets are held up behind the sheet so that their shadow falls on the sheet. The audience sits in front of the sheet. This is practised in Indonesia.

Use resources in the PNG School Journals wherever possible to construct similar exercises or other exercises which help students achieve the learning outcomes. The resources given in the Student Book will give students practice at changing text to instructions.

Student Book Chapter 6
Getting better in your reading

6.2.2 Revise and extend the range of skills used to improve reading speed, fluency and comprehension of text.

Sub-strand: Skills and Strategies acknowledging the importance of skills and strategies necessary to effectively communicate.

Indicator: students can recall previous knowledge of letter sounds and blends when reading unknown words.

Activity 1: Reading new words

Students will learn how to pronounce new words from listening to the teacher model them. However, it is also important that they learn some strategies for independent attempts. Activity 1 provides some strategies. You can add to these strategies. Model each of the examples given. Practise these skills and strategies and dictionary skills wherever there is an opportunity.

Indicator: use knowledge of alphabet when locating information independently.

Activity 2: Alphabet game

This is a sample of the kind of game you and your students can construct. The game can be made into a competition.

Indicator: students can locate different rhythm patterns in poetry and use them to assist fluent reading.

Activity 3: Patterns of sound

- Students read the poems to themselves, then to a partner. When they have gained confidence they can read to a group, and perhaps to the class.
- 'My country'—this poem/song has a swinging rhythm that students should enjoy. Discuss any unknown words.
- 'Flag song'—the rhythm is not as distinct in this song/poem. Students should be able to discover where the rhythm falters. Discuss patterns and let the students identify patterns that are important in their lives and the community.
- 'Traditional song'—traditional songs/poems do not have the same rhythm and pattern of sound because translation from the vernacular to English can destroy rhythm and sound patterns. Students should sing/chant traditional songs that they know. Decide if there is rhythm and sound patterns.
- 'Lizard'—the rhythm is not regular, but comes from repeated word patterns.
- Use any other poems you have that can illustrate rhythm and sound patterns.
- When doing the activity to count sounds in a line, have students beat each separate sound unit (syllable) on the desk and count them on their fingers. Note that some long words have only a single sound unit and some short words can have more than one sound unit.

Indicator: students can locate key words and phrases headings or sentences to use when summarising text.

Activity 4: Key words and phrases

- Students need to learn that some words in a sentence do more work than others. These are the words that if they were left out, the meaning of the sentence would be lost. When doing the activities, students may come up with answers that vary: apply the test above to find out if the words could be left out, while retaining meaning.
- Discuss what the other words do—they add information, and make it less work for the reader/listener.
- Discuss phrases—a small group of words that need to be part of a sentence in order to have meaning. On their own, they do not have meaning, though we can sometimes guess what the meaning is. We can use phrases on their own in a conversation where the context of the phrases makes their meaning clear, but they are not usually used on their own in formal writing.
- Students should work individually, and then test their shortened stories on a partner. Any differences should be discussed.

Activity 5: Perform a role play

The stories provide opportunities for role plays.

Activity 6: Reading for information

In reading for information, identifying the key words and phrases is an essential skill. This can later be used for note-taking.

Activity 7: Making a summary

- Summary making is a skill needed for project writing. Students need to learn how to extract information from a research source and put it into their own words. This involves making the source shorter by extracting the essential information.
- The questions in Activity 6 will help students check that they have the information necessary to make the summary. They should understand that the summary should take the ideas (and some facts) from the story and be expressed in their own words. No sentences should be copied from the original. Do not allow students to refer back to the original.

Indicator: students can predict the story that follows a newspaper headline and then compare it with the actual article.

Activity 8: Listing headings

Use predicting skills. Cover the lower part of the page while doing Question 1 and Question 2.

Activity 9: Writing a summary

Use the skills learnt in Activity 5 and 6.

Activity 10: Predicting the story

- Further practice in predicting. Students should begin individually then compare their predictions with partners and a group. Students should ask their partners 'Why did you predict that' to develop their skills of picking out main ideas.
- Provide further examples from the newspapers.

Indicator: the students can demonstrate, when reading, how the meaning of text can change when, for example, question, exclamation, or speech marks and commas are used.

- Punctuation can affect our interpretation of text.

Activity 11: Reading and writing with punctuation

- Revise punctuation.
- In pairs students find and identify each punctuation mark in the first part of the story. They should discuss what work the punctuation mark is doing and what meaning that punctuation mark gives to the sentence it is in.

Student Book Chapter 7
Are you reading a story? Are you reading facts?

6.2.3 Identify plot, character and themes in literary texts and how information and vocabulary are used in factual texts from PNG and other countries.

Sub-strand: Context and Text refers to the importance of learning and using language in different situations and the fact that how we communicate influences the kind of text we use.

Indicator: students can identify when a story is about an imaginary world and retell how the writer creates this for the reader.

Students need to know what is real and what is not in order to make informed decisions about the world around them.

Activity 1: Real or not?

- Students should be able to pick out elements of the *Coconut City* story which are obviously not real.
- Go over each of the elements of an imaginary story. Ask students to provide their own examples from traditional stories or other stories they have read.

Indicator: students can identify ways that characters, situations and problems in texts connect to their own experiences, thought and feelings.

- Your students bring information and feelings to the texts they read and these affect their way of looking at the text.

Activity 2: Things found in an imaginary story

Students should try to see connections between the elements of the story and characters they know in real life, the kind of conflicts that they experience or see around them, and the kind of action taken, and the resolution of the conflict through action.

Activity 3: Summarising plot to draw a story board

Answers to the questions are used along with skills learnt in Chapter 6 to make a summary of the plot.

Indicator: students can identify and describe recurring themes where appropriate, in stories of other cultures, relationships, place, time.

Activity 4: Themes

➢ After identifying themes in *Coconut City*, discuss each of the themes. These are called *universal themes* and students should be able to find examples of each theme in real-life stories they know. Groups can discuss the different themes. They are important in reading and could be displayed in the classroom.

➢ It is important that students can separate the plot from the theme, the action from the message.

➢ Plot can be shown through drawing a cause-and-effect chart.

Activity 5: What do you think of the story?

Students are being asked to think beyond the plot of the story and extend the ideas into their own lives.

Indicator: students can improvise a different ending to a story.

Activity 6: Finding a story

This activity can help students analyse the story, and indicate to the teacher that they have understood the elements of the story, especially plot and theme.

➢ Each of the possible endings should be discussed by the groups. Students in a group should make a choice of ending which they think best fits the plot and theme. When the choice has been made groups should plan out the new ending.

Activity 7: Write your own ending

➢ Students write their own endings following group discussion. The new ending should be added to students' writing portfolios.

For you to try: teachers need to provide many stories for students to practise these skills.

Indicator: students can read a non-fiction extract and review what further information is needed and where this could be obtained.

➢ Students need to analyse the facts in factual stories and try to think of what other facts would help their understanding of the stories.

Activity 8: True or imaginary?

➢ This is a true story. Scientific facts are given to back up the points made in the story. The indicator above practises an important skill students need for future life—that is knowing where to go to find out information they need. Take the opportunity to visit the library and find out about archaeology in PNG and other parts of the world. Students should try to find out if any archaeological excavations have been done in your area and, if possible, visit the site.

➢ Are there any traditions of old tools no longer used? What has happened to them? They should try to relate the story to their own community.

➢ Refer to the *Oxford PNG Primary School Atlas*

pages 48 and 49 ('Past'). Detailed information about excavations at Kuk, Western Highlands (a similar situation) can be found in the *Oxford PNG Secondary Atlas* pages 52 and 53.

- Students will practise summary-making skills again.
- Discuss the elements of plot, character, theme, setting, conflict and resolution in terms of a factual story. Which of them are relevant to a factual story?

Activity 9: Comparing an imaginary and a true story

This activity summarises the differences between the elements of factual and imaginary stories.

Activity 10: Questions about 'The Oldest Spade'

Question 6 asks the students to give an opinion.

Activity 11: Ending a factual story

Students again practise interpretive skills that allow them to change the ending of stories. Follow the same procedure as in Activities 6 and 7.

Activity 12: What do you think of the story?

Three groups (of six or nine) should be given one topic each. They should prepare an answer to be presented to the class. If Question 3 is not relevant to your area find out what students know in general.

Indicator: students can use words, fact and opinion, and begin to distinguish the difference in reading.

Activity 13: Is it fact or opinion?

Students have been expressing opinions about poems and stories. They should understand that different people have different opinions. They can accept the opinions of others if reasons are given for opinions. Opinions that have no basis in fact are personal points of view or personal preferences, and can lead to bias and stereotyping. If they wish to state an opinion themselves, they should realise the need to have some facts on which to base their own opinions.

Activity 14: Understanding the story

Students should analyse the parts of the story that show the story structure. Refer to story plans previously discussed.

Summary activities

Activity 15: Answer these questions

This is a summary activity and could be used for assessment.

Activity 16: What else would you like to know?

This is a further activity on research skills.

Activity 17: Ending the story

This could be used for assessment.

Student Book Chapter 8
Your turn to think about what you read

6.2.4 Respond to a range of literary and factual texts, while considering own experiences and those of their community.

Sub-strand: Critical Literacy acknowledges that language learners and users need to think beyond content and recognise and evaluate the beliefs that influence texts.

Indicators: students can compare and contrast a range of stories and justify preference; give an opinion about a dilemma faced by a character in

Reading

a story and discuss views on whether the author's solution is convincing.

Activity 1: Talking about stories

This activity applies to the following six stories. Some are fiction, some are fact. Add any other stories you have available. Students should have time to do the *three stage approach* to reading (before, during and after) for each story. This approach is outlined at the beginning of 'Teacher information' in this chapter.

- Have students read the stories and answer the questions in preparation for making a choice. Reading could include reading aloud following skills learnt in the Speaking and Listening chapters.
- They should remember what they have learnt about giving opinions in Chapter 6 and be prepared to back up (**justify**) their choice.
- Students need to *think beyond content and recognise and evaluate the beliefs that influence texts.* The author's beliefs have led to the solutions proposed by the author. Do they agree? They need to think about their own beliefs and recognise that their own beliefs may influence their response to texts.

Activity 2: Talking about ideas in 'Stories From the Past'

Two extra questions specifically for *Stories from the Past*. The full story is in *Climbing Mountains*, OUP, The Pacific Series.

Activity 3: Talking about ideas in 'Si Kabayan and the Snails'

Answers: Question 1—everyone but Si Kabayan.

- Question 2—Should say yes.
- Questions 3 and 4—students' answers will be based on values held in their own communities.
- Students need to think about how their own society is changing and how some of the old ideas about sharing and taking care of others are being weakened. What beliefs does the author of the story hold that could have influenced the text? Although this story is set in another country, the social problems are similar. There are other similar stories in the Grade 5 Reader *Tales of Si Kabayan*. Students can write a response paragraph and put it in their writing portfolio.

Activity 4: Talking about ideas in 'Working Hard, Selling Produce'

Answers: Question 1—Pauline does.

- Question 2—She has educated her children and supported the family.
- the role of women in their communities—is this the same as their traditional role, or is the role of women changing?
- Students can write a response paragraph and put it in their writing portfolio. What beliefs does their community hold that would colour their view of this story?

Activity 5: Talking about ideas in 'The Wrong Choice'

Students will have differing opinions and view points about the choices and dilemmas in this story. After discussion (and perhaps debate), students can write a response paragraph and put it in their writing portfolio. What beliefs does their community hold that would colour their view of this story? What beliefs does the author of the story hold that could have influenced the text? Where do these beliefs come from? (For example, are they influenced by the church they belong to?)

Activity 6: Talking about ideas in 'Cuscus Loves its Tea'

The story can lead to a discussion about cruelty to animals—is it cruel to make a wild animal dependent on humans?

Activity 7: Talking about ideas in 'The Science Experiment'

Answers: Question 1—students should decide for themselves—it would seem that Mrs Kuman actually punished them by telling them to do something they wanted to do anyway.

- Question 2—yes; show the link between what they learn in Social Science and how the boys applied their knowledge.
- Question 3 and 4—how can your students follow the boys' example?

Indicator: students can look up the same reference in two non-fiction source texts and compare the helpfulness and presentation of the information given.

Activity 8: Finding out about something

- Decide on the headings you will give your students for their research. Students can do research following reading other stories. Check that you have available resources for them to use for their research.
- The research is used to develop speaking skills.

Indicator: students can identify a moral or cultural issue in a locally relevant written text and present an improvised drama of an alternative way of dealing with the problem.

Activity 9: Important ideas in stories

Filling in the table will help students focus on the moral and cultural issues contained in the stories. (Story 1 *Stories from the Past* is not included on the table.)

Activity 10: Making a play

- A major step is considering the way the problems have been dealt with by the authors of the stories and developing an opinion about how they were dealt with. There are other ways to deal with most problems. It is important for students to come to realise that other people may not feel the same as they do about problems and their solutions.
- Guide them towards seeking an alternative method of dealing with the problems. Their plays should reflect this alternative way of dealing with the problem in each story.
- Teachers should also look out for articles in the newspaper that can be used. For example, articles about AIDS victims, providing food for hungry children in the towns, tourists looking at dried dead bodies.

Indicator: students can read a range of poems and recognise those which are contemporary by identifying up-to-date vocabulary/themes/issues.

Activity 11: Thoughts about poems

The general instructions apply to each of the poems. The answers to specific questions at the end of each poem can be found in Appendix 6. However, many of the questions ask for students' personal responses and do not have right or wrong answers. Students will enjoy poetry if they feel they have a personal right to respond to poems in their own way. All students' views about poetry should be considered valuable. As a teacher you can ask students to justify strong opinions about poems, but you must accept that sometimes you and some students will disagree.

Additional activities:

1. Students can respond to the poems by writing their own poetry.
2. Poems should be used for Speaking and Listening activities.
3. Situations in the poems can be used for role play.
4. Poems can be changed to prose text.

Writing

About this strand

In the four chapters of this strand, students will practise activities that lead to development of writing skills. When teaching writing skills teachers need to keep in mind the language principles stated in the *Language Teachers Guide.* For the writing strand they are that the principles of writing are based on the belief that all students need opportunities to:

- write every day, (as part of Language or another part of the curriculum),
- learn to write by writing (the teacher's role is not to talk about writing, but to provide many opportunities for students to do writing),
- learn to write by talking about their writing (students should discuss their writing in pairs or groups and with the teacher),
- learn to write following models of different types of genre,
- be aware of the many different contexts and purposes of writing that are used in the real world,
- see teachers using the writing process as part of their teaching,
- have their own and other class members' writing displayed around them to create a 'print rich environment',
- have positive feedback about their progress in writing tasks,
- have time in the class to go through the whole process of writing without pressure to complete 'the product',
- have time in the classroom to share their completed writing with other students,
- to be allowed to have some responsibility for the way their writing skills are developing (for example, if they can assess their own needs for paragraph development skills, they should be allowed to refine those skills with extra tasks),
- think about the writing process,
- write for different purposes, and
- write for real audiences (for readers outside the classroom).

(Based on *Language Teachers Guide*, page 6.)

Two key skills and processes for teaching writing are the **writing process** and using **genres**. These are outlined the *Language Teachers Guide,* page 11. The Student Book Chapter 9 guides students through the writing process.

Skills in using different genres are developed in all Language strands. In the writing strand, teachers should follow the four-step process (this also applies to oral use of the genres), on page 11 of the *Language Teachers Guide*. Activities in this four-step guide are covered in the other strands, demonstrating that writing cannot be taught in isolation.

Each chapter in the writing strand covers one of the outcomes for writing. The outcomes can be used to measure students' achievements in creating meaning in written language. The indicators are samples of the kind of activity you can plan to allow you to see if the outcome has been reached. The indicators given in the syllabus have been used as a basis for activities in the Student Book. Many of the writing activities in the Student Book are integrated with speaking and listening and reading in both Language and other subjects. You can plan other activities that can be used as indicators of the students' achievement of the outcome.

The activities and materials in the Student Book are not divided into lessons. You, as a teacher, will decide on the outcome to be taught and then select material for that outcome. Some material may be from different Language strands. The templates in the Appendix will help teachers use the Student Book and this book.

Key words

These are words that you as a teacher, and your students, will be using in the four chapters of the Writing strand (in order of use in the Student Book). You will find an explanation of the words in the Glossary in Appendix 7.

Student Book Chapter 9

writing process free writing plan draft edit habit routine usually tips letter

Student Book Chapter 10

strategies work of words adjective synonym verb tense capital letter full stop exclamation mark question mark comma speech mark

Student Book Chapter 11

journal autobiography personal letter business letter essay

Student Book Chapter 12

weak and strong words personal preference

Links to other main subjects

Student Book Chapter 9

Mask making: Creative art.

Scientific explanations: Science.

Student Book Chapter 10

Whales: Science.

Letter writing, asking for information: Social Science skill.

Student Book Chapter 11

Journal, keeping tradition: Social Science

Student Book Chapter 12

Issues are relevant to Social Science, Personal Development, Making a Living.

Possible assessment tasks

Tests for Student Book Chapter Nine

In Chapter 9 students learn about writing descriptions, their ideas, stories, poems, plays and advertisements. They will put a lot of things into their writing portfolios from the activities in the Speaking and Listening strand and the Reading strand. More will be added to the portfolio with activities in this strand.

The *Language Teachers Guide* (pages 46 and 47) provides some ideas about assessing writing. The suggested areas for assessment are:

- analysis of unassisted writing samples,
- process for unassisted writing sample,
- text summaries,
- teacher designed writing tasks,
- negotiated lists of criteria,
- journals, diaries and drafts,
- spelling checklists and
- a general criteria sheet framework.

Teachers will assess writing across all the Language strands and other curriculum areas.

For assessment in this strand teachers will provide students with appropriate writing tasks. When they have done the tasks, students should think about what they have learnt, and fill in the table below. Teachers can also use the tables as assessment guides. As teachers, you will use some of these things to help you know how well your students are writing and students can see what they can do to make their writing better.

(Note: This table can be adjusted so that students can grade their self-assessment as good, needs improvement etc.)

Ask the students to fill in this table. Students should tick off the things they think they are learning to do.

I am learning the steps of the writing process.	
I am getting better at using the writing process.	
I am learning to know the kinds of words to use if I am writing about an ordinary day.	
I am learning to know how to put events in order.	
I am learning to know how to use time order words.	
I am learning to know how to put feelings in stories.	
I am learning to know that putting details in stories makes them interesting.	
I am learning to know what to write about if I want to describe a person.	
I am learning to know what to write about if I want to describe a place.	
I am learning to know where to start and the order to describe things.	
I am learning to know what kind of words to use when I write an advertisement.	
I am learning to know how to make a story exciting by using my imagination.	
I am learning to know the kinds of words to use for writing instructions.	
I am learning to know that instructions must be very clear.	
I am learning to know that I must write the steps of instructions in order.	
I am learning to know the kinds of words to use when I am writing an explanation.	
I am learning to know the kinds of words to use when I am writing my opinion.	

Tests for Student Book Chapter Ten

In Chapter 10 students practise some of the skills needed to make their writing more accessible to the reader, such as correct spelling and paragraph structure.

1. Check the spelling of these words in the dictionary. Write the correct spelling.

aniversary, generetion, drougth, burgular, recieve, cheif, holesale, audiance, arguement, aplikation.

Writing

Answers: anniversary, generation, drought, burglar, receive, chief, wholesale, audience, argument, application

2. Write what work the underlined words in the sentences do:

1. I asked the headmaster if I could go <u>home</u> early.
2. That is a <u>pretty</u> hibiscus in your hair.
3. I <u>feel</u> sick today.
4. Why <u>is</u> the dog <u>running</u> away?
5. The teapot is <u>full</u>.
6. The <u>pawpaw</u> is ripe.

Answers:

1. noun: it names the place where the student wants to go.
2. adjective: it gives more information about the noun.
3. present tense verb: it gives the action.
4. continuous tense verb: it tells that the action is happening at the present time.
5. adjective: it tells more about the noun.
6. noun: it tells what the verb and adjective refer to, it is the *subject* of the sentence, or what the sentence is about.

3. Write a paragraph about selling food at the market. Put in adjectives to make the paragraph interesting. Make some of the sentences in the present tense, some in the past tense and some in the future tense. Put some dialogue in the story and make sure to use correct punctuation.

Ask the students to fill in this checklist when they have written and discussed the paragraph and the checklist with the teacher. Teachers can use this checklist to assess the paragraph.

Checklist:

The paragraph begins with a sentence (topic sentence) which clearly tells the reader what the paragraph will be about.	
The following sentences in the paragraph all give more information about the topic. (They develop the topic indicated in the topic sentence.)	
Adjectives are used.	
Different tenses are used.	
Dialogue is used.	
Correct punctuation is used.	

4. Use these phrases in sentences:

1. at the beach
2. to the market
3. after the rain
4. next to Leilani
5. the following day

Tests for Student Book Chapter Eleven

In Chapter 11 students learn how to find the different parts of writing and to do some writing of their own.

Teachers will give their students some writing tasks to do. When the students have done them, they should think about what they have learnt, and fill in the table below. Teachers can also use the tables as assessment guides. As teachers, you will use some of these things to help you know how well your students are writing and students can see what they can do to make their writing better. (Note: This table can be adjusted so that students can grade their self-assessment.)

Ask the students to fill in this table. Students should tick off the things they think they are learning to do.

I am learning that there are many different reasons for writing.	
I am learning that I need to know what is my reason for writing.	
I am learning that there are many different audiences for writing.	
I am learning that I need to know who is the audience for my writing.	
I am learning how to write a journal.	
I am learning that there are three main parts to stories.	
I am learning how to write an autobiography.	
I am learning that there are different kinds of letters.	
I am learning how to write some different kinds of letters.	
I am learning how to plan an essay.	
I am learning about the different types of paragraphs in essays.	
I am learning how to write a good paragraph.	

Tests for Student Book Chapter Twelve

In Chapter 12 students learn how to make their writing strong and how to give their own opinions.

1. Match the weak verbs in column A with the strong words in column B. Students should use the dictionary if they are not sure of the meanings of words.

look bright	swirl
the horse ran	soar
care for	amble
walk	glisten
revolve	nurture
fly	galloped

Answers in order: glisten, galloped, nurture, amble, swirl, soar

Give your students a variety of writing tasks that involve expression of a point of view. Following the task the students should fill in the table below. You can use the table to help you assess how well the student is writing. Students can use the table to locate areas in which they need to improve.

Ask the students to fill in this table. Tick off the things you think you are learning to do.

I am learning that strong words make my writing easier to understand and more interesting.	
I am learning that people have different opinions about many things in life.	
I am learning that there are reasons why people have different points of view.	
I am learning that I can give my point of view when I have strong feelings about something.	
I am learning that my audience will take more notice of my point of view if I can give reasons for it and examples.	
I am learning that it is important to know some facts that support my point of view.	
I am learning that stereotypes and bias do not help people agree with my point of view.	

Teacher information

In this section you will find information on the activities and background to some activities in the four chapters of the Writing strand. The information is for you to use, if you wish, in helping you plan your lessons.

The *Language Teachers Guide* (pages 28 to 31) provides writing strategies for the teacher to use in teaching writing. These can be applied to the activities in the Student Book. The topics covered are dictagloss, journal writing and paragraph writing (including grammar).

You will find the answers to Student Book Activities in Appendix 6.

Student Book Chapter 9
Some different kinds of writing

6.3.1 Plan and produce a range of literary and factual texts for a range of purposes and audiences.

Sub-strand: Production—to provide opportunities for students to use language for real purposes.

Indicators: students can use the process of planning, drafting, rehearsing, editing and publishing to compose texts; write descriptions of places, people and events; draft simple character sketches.

The writing process

The *Language Teachers Guide* (page 11) gives an eleven-step process. There are many different ways of outlining the writing process. However, all of them stress the need for ample planning, research and rewriting. All stages of the process can be assessed in terms of student outcomes, as well as the finished product.

Students should use the process for any kind of writing they do (in Language and other curriculum areas), adapting it to the requirements of the genre.

Step 1: If the topic is not being supplied by the

teacher, an additional part of this step is student generation of a topic. Students should be urged to write about something they know at least a little about as this gives them a starting point. Following their brainstorming (free writing), they can do some research to add to their knowledge of the topic.

Brainstorming can be done by individuals, pairs, groups or the whole class, with the teacher recording the results on the blackboard. Brainstorming can be completely free, with the results recorded in an unorganised manner. Or there can be a degree of control with linked ideas being grouped.

Step 2: This step applies to writing tasks that need facts and information. An imaginary story does not usually require the student to do research.

Step 3: Students use what they know about purpose and audience. The plan they make will reflect the genre being used.

Step 4: You can provide 'frameworks' for different types of genres. Several of the genres discussed in other strands of the Student Book have this information in the right hand column (see the story 'My School Days').

Stress the importance of a well-thought out plan.

Step 5: A good plan will make the writing of the first draft easier for the student. Remind students that they will be re-writing this material. Students should focus on getting their ideas written down in the order they want them to be.

Step 6: If possible, it is best to leave the first draft for a while and to return to it with fresh eyes. The student is more likely to see their own mistakes in this way and not to rely on peers or teachers to find problems for them.

The final copy produced by the student should be the result of at least one re-writing. It should be following any guidelines given by the teacher, and free of errors.

Activity 1: Talking about an ordinary day

- Model for writing about an ordinary day: 'My School Days'.
- Students read the story about a child's ordinary day. Note that this and other stories in Chapter 9 are extracts. Students could be asked to predict what happens next in the story, and how the story might end.
- Discuss the ideas of regularly done activities, 'habit' and 'routine'. Explain that 'usually' does not mean every time, but most of the time, more often than not.
- After individuals fill in the table for a usual school day, they should compare with a partner and discuss similarities and differences.

Activity 2: Getting ready to write a story about an ordinary day

- Model for writing about an ordinary day: 'My School Days'
- Students can use this as a basis for a group discussion. Groups should report on the kinds of things their members usually do. Build up a generalised plan on the blackboard.

For you to try: students follow the appropriate steps of the writing process. In this case, they have the topic, and have done some brainstorming about information that will be needed in the writing.

- At this stage, they need to think of how many paragraphs their story will need (such as: introduction, early morning, on the way to school, school hours, going home, before the evening meal, after the evening meal, conclusion).
- During editing they should check on use of signal words.
- The tips are designed to give some hints about improvement. Students should read them and use them as part of their editing process.

Activity 3: Getting ready to write a story about a character

➢ Model for writing about a character: 'My Uncle Sigin'

➢ Students should relate the ideas listed to the parts of the model.

For you to try: the story should include the suggestions. Students need to put in their feelings and to demonstrate why they chose that character.

➢ The model poem can be followed, or students can use any other structure for a poem.

Activity 4: Getting ready to write a story about a place

➢ Model for writing about a place: 'My Place'.

➢ In some writing, the setting becomes a very important part of the story. In the model, the setting almost seems like a character.

➢ Students should relate the points in Activity 4 and the points in 'For you to try' to the structure of the story. For example, students can work in pairs to find and describe the parts of the story which describe the landscape closest to the favourite place, and further away.

➢An extension activity can be to draw a map from the model.

For you to try: students should include their feelings.

Indicator: students can write logical recounts of personal experiences, literary simple texts, procedures, explanation.

Activity 5: Getting ready to write a story about something that happened to you

➢ Model for writing a story about something that happened to you: 'The Day of the Gumi Race'.

➢ Pair or group discussion will help students choose a topic for their story. They should comment (in a polite manner) on whether they think the topics chosen by others are suitable.

For you to try: students should use narrative form. The story they choose should be something special that happened to them, that is important to them, or memorable in some way. This will enable them to conclude with a comment about why the story is important.

➢ Stress that although this is based on a true event, students can use their imaginations to make events more interesting by exaggerating the excitement. Dialogue should be included.

➢ Students can write a drama of the story 'The Day of the Gumi Race' or of their own story.

Activity 6: Getting ready to write some instructions

➢ Model for writing about how to do something: 'Making a mask for a play'.

➢ Students should analyse the framework of the model and use it to plan their own instructions.

➢ Pair or group discussion should show the students whether they have picked a topic that they know enough about for instruction writing. If the student is unable to show that they have sufficient knowledge, direct them to another topic. Steps should be discussed before the instructions are written.

For you to try: if the teacher is satisfied that the student can write complete instructions they can follow the ideas and tips.

Activity 7: Getting ready to write an explanation

➢ Model for writing about how to explain something: 'What are Stars?'.

➢ Students should be aware of the difference between an explanation about how to do something (instructions) and an explanation which describes something.

- Discuss the plan shown in the right hand column of the model. What are the parts of the plan? What purpose do they have?
- The topic suggested ('The Moon') can be used by students. However, teachers can direct students to other topics that are relevant to other curriculum areas.

For you to try: information and a diagram on which to base the explanation are given.

- Students should follow the plan given in the model.

Indicator: express an opinion in a letter to a named reader.

Activity 8: Getting ready to write your opinion

- Model for writing about your opinion: 'A simple answer'.
- Begin with a discussion of the model. Students discuss other topics to express some opinions. They should use what they have learnt in Speaking and Listening to disagree politely.

For you to try: students can choose their own topics or you can provide topics relevant to your community.

- Note on facts: opinions are more likely to be listened to if they have facts to back them up. In the example, *many of our roads are very bad*, the facts are provided by the frequently published photographs of bad roads. Although this is a fact it is also a generalisation based on observation.
- The following two indicators are incorporated into Chapters 11 and 12.

Indicator: students can compose a range of imaginative factual and critical texts; compose a range of imaginative texts including narratives, poetry, scripts and advertisements.

Student Book Chapter 10
Making your writing better

6.3.2 Apply knowledge of sentence structure, grammatical features, punctuation conventions and spelling strategies to refine students' own writing.

Sub-strand: Skills and Strategies acknowledging the importance of skills and strategies necessary to effectively communicate.

Indicators: students can sound out and spell using knowledge of letter sounds and blends; spell by analogy with known words.

Activity 1: Ways to help you spell

After individually filling in the table, groups can discuss the usefulness of the strategies. The techniques can be ranked per group. Teachers and students can add to the list.

Activity 2: Using some of the ways to learn how to spell

Extend this activity by having students do dictionary research to find other words that have small words inside them.

Activity 3: Using what you know about letters that often go together

This activity is a sample of the kinds of letter blends students will be familiar with. Further exercises on letter blends are in the Pacific Series *Using English,* Grade 6, Books 1—3, OUP, and *Improve Your Spelling Skills* (Literacy Skills for Papua New Guinea, Susan Baing, OUP).

Activity 4: Checking spelling using your dictionary

Groups discuss what ways they use when they want to find a word they don't know how to spell in the dictionary. Summarise any strategies suggested by students and rank them according to usefulness.

Activity 5: Checking what kind of word it is

Dictionary and grammar skills.

Activity 6: Checking meaning

Dictionary and grammar skills.

Indicator: students can discuss how adjectives give more information about or describe a noun.

Activity 7: The work of words in a sentence

- Students need to discover that the form of a word does not always reveal the work the word does in a sentence. For example *cut* has the same form for *noun* and *verb*.
- Students can search the dictionary for similar words.
- Teachers can extend this activity by students writing their own sentences for group or pair analysis.

Activity 8: Using the right adjective

Students match adjectives and nouns. They can make a similar 'game' for their group.

Activity 9: Using adjectives

- Students use the information about order of adjectives to write sentences. They should search available books to find sentences with multiple adjectives and check out the order. Here are some sentences they could practise on. Students write the sentence then write above each adjective the category of adjective it is:
- I have two, square, blue boxes.
- Jack took the small, fat, black dog to the river.
- There was a large, round, green teapot on the shelf.

Note: There are other categories of adjective such as quality or degree and the order is not always fixed. The order given in the Student Book is one of the acceptable ways of ordering adjectives. However, your students' search may come up with exceptions to this order.

Activity 10: Adding adjectives to make writing more interesting

Note that students should avoid using strings of meaningless adjectives and use only adjectives that add something to the picture.

For example: The three happy ~~little~~ children…

Indicator: students can include synonyms in writing.

Activity 11: Using synonyms

The English language has many words with similar meanings. Here are some rules for using synonyms.

1. The synonym is always the same part of speech as the word it replaces
2. Take care that you don't change the meaning too much (the words have similar meanings, but they are not exactly the same: quarrel, argument, disagreement, row, squabble).
3. Use synonyms to make your meaning clear and as precise as possible (The boy was *sturdy* in build. Do you mean muscular, strong, heavy…)
4. Use a short word rather than a long word.
5. Use a familiar word rather than an unfamiliar or 'impressive' one.

Indicator: students can use a range of verbs and different tenses in writing.

Activity 12: Writing present tense

Two forms of the present tense are given. Make sure students know the difference.

Activity 13: Changing present tense to past tense

- This is a skill needed for forming reported speech.
- The activity can be extended by having students in pairs write present tense sentences to be changed by their partner.

Activity 14: Using future tense

There are a number of ways to express future.

Writing good sentences:

These activities use skills and strategies. Discuss the sentences and phrases. Why is one group of words a sentence and another group of words not a sentence?

Activity 15: Are these sentences?

Students should discuss the reasons for their decisions. For example:

1. Joe sat by the river. This is a sentence because the reader **has** all the information they need to understand the meaning.
2. To hear her tell the story. This is a **not** sentence because the reader **does not have** all the information they need to understand the meaning.

Activity 16: Using different kinds of sentences

This activity stresses the key element of sentences, that they must carry meaning for the reader or listener. Sometimes this meaning is conveyed by context, as in a dialogue.

Activity 17: Making phrases into sentences

- Unlike the dialogue sentence, a phrase does not stand on its own. Phrases add information to a sentence.

Indicator: students can use punctuation correctly in writing.

- This section considers only capital letters, full stops, commas, question marks and exclamation marks. Dialogue punctuation is given separately. Punctuation adds meaning to writing. If punctuation is used wrongly, it can change meaning or make meaning difficult to understand.

Activity 18: Adding capital letters and full stops

Students should be looking for meaning.

Activity 19: Adding commas

Students should be looking for meaning.

Dialogue punctuation:

These are the basic rules. There are other rules which students may find examples of when they read.

Activity 20: Punctuating a dialogue

Students have used dialogue in writing narrative.

Editing:

Students need to consider spelling, punctuation, good sentence writing, verb form.

Student Book Chapter 11
Looking at how people write in different ways

6.3.3 Identify how texts have been structured to suit the context.

Sub-strand: Context and Text refers to the importance of learning and using language in different situations and the fact that how we communicate influences the kind of text we use.

Indicator: students can discuss reasons why people write.

Activity 1: Think about why and what you write

- ➢ Students fill in the table with the kinds of writing that they personally do. The purposes will be those appropriate to their lives.
- ➢ Students should find that they write because they need to communicate meaning to a reader (audience).

Activity 2: Thinking about why other people write

Students need to recognise that all writers have purpose. They should consider what they have recently read and try to find the writers' purposes.

Activity 3: Thinking about the audience

Purpose and audience are closely linked. If the writing is not aimed correctly at the target audience, the purpose will be lost. They should realise that audiences can be individuals or large groups of people.

Activity 4: More about the different kinds of writing

Students will write a summary of what they have learnt about the writing process.

Indicator: students can compose own texts that use and explore their own experiences, thoughts and feelings.

Model for writing a journal: 'Journal'.

- ➢ Students should be encouraged to write journals.

For you to try: entries in journals can be very short, or can extend for several pages. Some very famous people wrote journals and these have been published for us to read. While no one but the students might read the journal, they should be encouraged to write correctly.

Indicators: students can study parts of a text and explain their functions; demonstrate their knowledge of the ways certain genres and their structures and features suit particular purposes, audiences and situations.

Activity 5: Asking questions about how stories work

Students can refer to any story in the Student Book, or other stories they have recently read.

For you to try: students follow the pattern of narrative.

Activity 6: About the story

- ➢ Model for writing an autobiography: 'My Life So Far'.
- ➢ Answer these questions about autobiography. Students should be thinking about the plan or framework that shows the structure of this and other pieces of writing.

For you to try: students will write about their own lives until the present. Some topics will be generalised, but there should also be some specific incidents.

Activity 7: Talking about letters

- ➢ Make sure students talk about purpose and audience.

Model: A personal letter

- ➢ Students discuss the parts, who they think the audience is, what the purpose is.

For you to try: as this is a personal letter, informal words and sentence structure can be used.

Model: Business letter

- ➢ Students discuss the observable differences between the personal and business letters.
- ➢ Students discuss the kinds of business letters they know about.

➢ Get samples of business letters for class display.

For you to try: students will write a similar letter asking for information.

Parts of a basic essay

Discuss what students know about essays.

➢ Here are some basic types of essay:

1. to give reasons for something (account for)
2. to break something down into its parts and examine each part (analyse)
3. to show a point of view (argue)
4. to look at how things are similar (compare)
5. to look at how things are different (contrast)
6. to give a detailed account in your own words (describe)
7. to show how something changes (development)
8. to give the meaning of (explain)
9. to explain in what way something happens (how)
10. to show in what ways something is important (significance)
11. to give reasons for something (why).

Purpose of essays:

1. to entertain the reader
2. to give information
3. to show you understand a text
4. to explain how something is done.

Model for writing an essay:

'Why Playing Sport Is Good For Us'.

➢ Students identify the three parts of the model essay.

➢ Discuss the framework in the right-hand column.

Activity 8: Writing paragraphs

➢ Follow the model and analyse the remaining two body paragraphs.

For you to try: write a paragraph following the basic pattern.

➢ As students become more confident writers, they can break away from this pattern.

For you to try: write an essay following the framework.

➢ As students become more confident writers, they can break away from this pattern.

Student Book Chapter 12
Your turn to think about what you write

6.3.4 Respond to own writing, while considering own experiences and those of the community.

Sub-strand: Critical Literacy acknowledges that language learners and users need to think beyond content and recognise and evaluate the beliefs that influence texts.

Indicator: students can compose texts that present different points of view.

Discuss points of view, personal opinions, opinions about important issues. Students should realise the difference between a personal preference and a point of view. A personal preference is, for example, that you prefer eating pineapple to mango, or that soccer is a better sport to play than basketball.

Activity 1: Sorting out points of view

Students will need to think carefully about each statement before deciding if it is a positive (in favour of) or negative (against) view. They will need to explain the statements and their decision about the statements. Allow time for students to explore the options. People from the community could be asked to contribute to the discussions.

Head tax

1. Everyone gets something from the government. We should give something back. *This statement is in favour of paying head tax, as a way of contributing to government funding.*
2. You have to pay for what you get. Head tax is away of paying for these things. *In favour: we get services; these services need to be paid for.*

3. Some people do not get anything from the government. They should not have to pay head tax. *This statement is against the paying of head tax. It argues that remote areas receive no services, so they should not have to help pay for other people's services.*
4. Some places have no schools or clinics. Why should people living there have to pay? *As above (3).*
5. If you have no way to make money, how can you pay? *Against paying head tax: pointing out that many people have no source of income, so the practicalities of collecting it would outweigh the benefits.*
6. How do we know the person collecting the head tax will give it to the LLG. *Against: questioning the methods of collecting.*
7. There are too many people who collect money for the wrong things and make promises. *Against: asking whether the population would believe they would benefit from head tax collection.*
8. Robbers could take the money. *Against: Why pay if the money won't reach where it is supposed to—based on personal experience of self or others.*
9. The government does not have enough money. We all need to give something. *In favour: practising self-reliance.*

Capital punishment

1. In other countries some people have been killed who did nothing wrong. *Against: the legal system can make mistakes. An innocent person can be executed. This has happened, but recent advances in DNA testing have released some prisoners from death row.*
2. The Bible say an eye for an eye, a tooth for a tooth. *In favour: the punishment must fit the crime: if you kill, you should be killed yourself.*
3. If you kill someone you should be killed too. *In favour: as above (2).*
4. A killer can be made into a better person in prison. *Against: the argument is that we all have some good inside us. A criminal could change for the better if given a chance.*
5. Judges can be wrong. *Against: As above (1).*

People without jobs going to villages

1. There is lots of land for people to grow gardens. *In favour of sending jobless people to villages: the argument is that they could work and be useful citizens there. The argument is a flawed generalisation, because not all parts of the country have ample garden land.*
2. Crime would go down in the towns. *In favour: another flawed generalisation—there is no guarantee that this would happen.*
3. Some places do not have enough land for more people. *Against: this is the other side of reason one. It is a true generalisation.*
4. Some land will get spoiled. *Against: As above (3).*
5. Many people in towns do not know their culture. *Against: the argument is that people who do not know their culture will find it hard to go home to the village. They might not fit in, and this could lead to trouble.*
6. Many people in towns have forgotten their traditional language. *Against: as above (5). A language barrier will make it hard to fit in.*
7. People would take new ideas. *In favour: new ideas are seen as a positive thing that would help development.*
8. Many people in towns don't know how to make gardens. *Against: these people would be a burden on village people.*
9. Many people in towns know how the government works. *In favour: they could help village people access funds and development.*

Activity 2: People have different points of view

- Most arguments have a clear opposing view. Students discuss the view given and break it down into a list of reasons supporting the point of view.
- They should then write a list of reasons showing the opposing point of view and from

that list write their own paragraph.

➢ This activity could be developed into a debate.

Activity 3: Groups with different points of view

This activity will lead towards a debate. The teacher will need to match two opposing groups on each topic.

Letters to the editor:

➢ The letters to the editor page in a newspaper is a common place for points of view to be expressed.

For you to try: students follow the model.

Activity 4: Reading someone's opinion

After reading the discussion essay 'Are Our Children Getting the Right Kind of Food?', students fill in the outline.

Activity 5: Questions about 'Longer Library Hours' for you to answer

Answers:

1. Many schools have libraries. Libraries are shut a lot of the time.
2. They are not open long enough—libraries should be open longer.
3. Reason 1—many students don't have books at home.
4. Reason 2—many students don't have a good place to study.
5. Yes—she looks at the disadvantages of longer hours.
6. She wants longer hours and gives some ideas about how this could be done.

For you to try: students should follow the models.

Indicator: identify the use of powerful verbs.

Activity 6: Using strong verbs

➢ Students can use dictionaries or thesauruses to locate more words.

➢ Any new words should be found in the dictionary, used for spelling, and be recorded with meanings in vocabulary books.

Activity 7: Making a poem stronger

➢ Students do vocabulary activities as above. Follow the model to replace verbs.

For you to try: If the poem 'The Flying Foxes' is unavailable, use another poem with strong verbs.

➢ Students can write the poem following models learnt in other chapters of the Student Book, or other models provided by the teacher.

Indicator: students can compose texts with characters that challenge typical stereotypes such as gender stereotypes.

➢ The three stories given all show characters which do not follow stereotypes.

For you to try: students have learnt about stereotypes in previous chapters. Revise the concept before they read the stories and write their own story.

Appendices

Appendix 1: Lesson planning table

Outcomes	Things to work from and plan for
1. Learning outcome	Identify the outcome in the curriculum that you are working from.
2. Content: topic or key concept	Base this on the outcome. Decide on a theme, from other curriculum areas if appropriate, for example, our local culture.
3. What will learners learn in the particular lessons?	How will learners achieve the learning outcome? • what knowledge will they learn? • what skills will they learn? • what values and attitudes will they adopt?
4. Number of lessons that need to be taught	How many lessons do you plan to teach on this particular topic?

Assessing progress	Things to think through
1. Evidence of learning	What you will look for in each learner's work? Write down the assessment objectives. (Each one should be something a learner can do.)
2. The way learning will be assessed	Examples of what procedures you may use: • formal (oral or written presentation) • informal (teacher observation) • small task within a larger project • homework • test

Classroom practice	Things to consider
1. Method or activity	What will you do and what will learners do, and in what sequence?
2. Time	For how long will you explain or model new concepts? For how long will learners do each activity?
3. Teaching methods	How exactly will you arrange learners? • as a whole group? • working in pairs? • working individually?
4. Resources needed	Where will learners be? • in the classroom? • outside? **List any resources you may need for students to complete tasks.**

Appendix 2: Yearly plan

Units of work	Term 1	Term 2	Term 3	Term 4
Speaking and listening	Outcome… Indicator…			
Reading				
Writing				

Appendix 3: Term plan

Week	Outcomes	Student tasks	Required resources	Assessment procedures
1–3				
4–6				
7–10				

Appendix 4: Lesson plan

Teaching group √	Required Materials
Individual Whole class Team group	
Learning Strategies	**Specific Content—lesson plan Collaborating**
Interpreting Predicting Planning √ Investigating Recording √ Justifying Changing Communicating √	
Curriculum Strand	**Assessment strategy**
Cross Curricula Strands	**Cross Curricula activities**

Appendix 5: Assessment strategies

Sample 1: Cognitive skills template

LEARNING SKILLS ASSESSMENT CHECKLIST

For assessing learning skills, group communication skills and attitudes

NAME: **DATE:**

Skills	Skills observed √	Comments
Learning skills • can form and ask questions • can follow instructions • can find information • can find required information • can express ideas clearly and correctly • can critically reflect on own work • can organise oneself efficiently • understands how to improve own work • manages use of time well		
Group Skills • follows group rules • works cooperatively within a team • contributes to discussions without dominating • listens while other people speak • accommodates different points of view		
Attitudes • respects other students' points of view • participates freely in activities • works in a constructive and positive way • values the beliefs held by other students		

Sample 2: Students' own assessment of their skills development

STUDENT SELF-ASSESSMENT CHECKLIST

NAME: **DATE:**

Skills	**√ Can do**
My Learning Skills • I can ask questions. • I can follow instructions. • I can find the information that I need. • I can express myself clearly and correctly. • I can think about what was right and wrong about my work. • I can work neatly. • I am well organised. • I understand how to improve my work. • I use my time well.	
My Group Skills • I can work well with others in a group. • I can listen when others are talking. • I can discuss something without getting angry.	
My Attitude • I can listen and respect what others have to say. • I can take responsibility for my own work. • I can share in a group activity. • I can learn from my mistakes.	

My Comment

Appendix 6: Answers to activities in the Student Book

Student Book Chapter 1

Activity 3: Holim Pig

1. The first scene could be tribal fighting. Then a scene with discussion and decision making. Characters: fighters, leaders, narrator.
2. Setting: *In a village setting.* What would they say? *Fighting talk, followed by decision making.*
3. Scene: *In an arena.* Characters: *contestants, audience, pigs.* What would they say? *Boasting from contestants, pig noises, audience must say 'Holim Pig', narrator says final joke line.*

Activity 8: Expressions in stories

1. angry 2. frightened 3. worried 4. scared
5. lonely 6. happy 7. happy 8. pleased
9. happy

Student Book Chapter 3

Activity 1: Making sense

Correct sentences:

b) The woman with the baby is worried about her house.

d) The old man is thinking that his canoe is broken, so he can't go fishing.

Activity 4: A muddled conversation

b) 'It's something! No, it's nothing!' replied Manuai.

a) 'It could be, I suppose,' replied Manuai.

a) 'It's nothing. Don't yell like that! There are always fireflies around at this time of night!' replied Manuai.

b) 'Now you are really frightening me,' replied Manuai.

Activity 8: Muddled instructions

First of all you pass each leaf quickly through a fire. After that you boil it for a short time in fresh water. Next you take it out of the water and cut off the sharp edges of the middle part of the leaf with a shell or sharp knife. After cutting off the sharp edges you then put the strip of pandanus leaf in the sun for several days. Finally you roll the strips in long coils and leave them until they are needed.

Activity 11: Putting directions in the right order

Uncle Tau has taken some money out of the bank in Rewa Street. He wants to go to the Post Office to send the money to his daughter. He crosses Rewa Street and turns into Dika Street. He goes along Dika Street to the corner where the hotel is. He turns left at the corner, into Rowa Street. He crosses the road at the crossing. He walks along Rua Street to the corner of Kila Street. He goes into the Post Office by the door on Kila Street.

Student Book Chapter 4

Activity 1: Matching pictures and stories

1. Two boys, swimming, warning each other, exclamation marks. The words: Look behind you!
2. Member, Councillor, at a meeting, formal speech, formal names, listing of people.
3. Two people who don't know each other, in a village, one trying to find a particular place, asks for help.
4. Two boys who know each other are fishing, talking about finding fish, words they use, use names.
5. Father and son, in village, instructions for making something, uses names, gives steps and signals, uses command words.
6. Weather forecaster at radio or TV station, giving information, by the words used.

Activity 4: Talking when you do not agree

1. Called her dumb
2. 3 times
3. 3 times
4. He uses 'we' instead of 'you'.
5. Yes, he accuses her of not knowing how to cook rice and burning it.
6. No, he offers suggestions.
7. Conversation 2.
8. The others offer to help instead of making accusations.

Activity 4: Talking abut bias and stereotypes

The sentences all show bias and stereotyping.

Student Book Chapter 5

Activity 3: Plan of the story 'The Scary Watermelon'

Title: 'The Scary Watermelon'

Who: Singu; *Where*: in the village, in the watermelon garden; *When*: One afternoon.

Problem: how to stop the boys stealing without hurting them.

Events: (This is a suggestion—there could be differences.)

1. Singu decides to scare the children.
2. He watches the boys.
3. He finds the biggest melon and digs a hole.
4. He gets ready with his hat and flour.
5. He hides in the garden.
6. He waits and when the boys come, he moans.
7. He goes home happy.

Activity 5: Time Signals in 'Day Dreams'

That morning Hannah sat in the classroom. The air was very hot. She did not like maths. She tried to pay attention, but her mind started to wander. *Then* a dreamy look came over her face. She would imagine that she was walking through the cool forest. The forest was Hannah's favourite place. *Next* Hannah imagined she was walking along the path to the river…

But day dreams, like night dreams, do not always go the way we want. *Suddenly* Hannah felt her dress being pulled. Was it caught on a branch? No! She looked down and *then* she saw a ghostly hand coming out of the bushes. Hannah screamed out loud.

Next she heard a voice calling her name…

Hannah came out from under the desk. *Then* she looked around. She wasn't in the forest. There was no ghostly hand. All she saw was the other children staring at her and giggling. *At last* she realised she had been day dreaming…

Activity 8: How time passes in 'Cat Food'

Time Line for the story 'Cat Food'

Event	Time
Fishing	Thursday morning and afternoon
Arrived at canoe place	Thursday evening
Walked home	
Ran back	
Stood on snake	
Hit snake	
Father came	
Walked home together	
Went to canoe place	Friday morning
Tried to find snake	
Walked back to house	
Saw half-eaten snake	

Student Book Chapter 6

Activity 2: Alphabet game

chief and cough

Activity 3: Patterns of sound:

1. 'My country' Line 1 5 sounds
   Line 2 4 sounds Line 3 5 sounds
   Line 4 4 sounds Line 5 5 sounds
   Line 6 4 sounds Line 7 5 sounds
   Line 8 4 sounds
2. 'Flag Song' Verse 1: Line 1 8 sounds
   Line 2 10 sounds Line 3 9 sounds
   Line 4 9 sounds Line 5 9 sounds.
   Verse 2: Line 6 8 sounds Line 7 10 sounds
   Line 8 9 sounds Line 9 9 sounds
   Line 10 9 sounds.
3. Verse 1: 7, 7, 7, 3, Verse 2: 5, 7, 5, 3,
   Verse 3: 9, 10, 4
4. Lines 1 and 2, then Lines 4, 5, 6.

Activity 4: Key words and phrases

There will be various answers.

'Funny Fish' Bop and Anis went fishing in their canoe. They paddled a long way from the beach. Then they threw their lines in the water. Suddenly both boys felt a strong tug on their lines. They were excited and pulled the lines in. Oh dear! They found they had caught each other's lines and there was no big fish.

'Siwai Legend' Long ago Siwai people garamuts hollow stone. Friendship feast drums beaten.

Guests set off. Heard a strange noise. Orphan boy beating drum made from a hollow log. Better sound. Garamuts from hollow logs today.

Activity 6: Reading for information

'Storing Food' Cannot eat the food, must be stored. Store cool place. Cover the food. Foods from the store, tins with tight lids. Salt not be stored in a tin, rusty. Tinned food is opened. Not be left in the tin, put these things in another kind of container. Use tinned food as soon as possible after it is opened.

Activity 11: Reading and writing with punctuation

The night was very dark. There were no fire-flies on the path. They did not have a torch, only a smoky kerosene lamp that did not give much light. Suddenly they heard a low moaning noise in the trees on the left of the path in the direction of the magic cave.

'What was that?' whispered Serah.

'I don't know,' answered Gemboe

The moaning came again, louder this time.

'Run!' shouted Serah 'Don't wait to find out what it is!'

The two girls ran back down the track, tripping and scraping their knees. From behind the bushes came two boys, Serah's brothers.

'That will teach Serah to doubt our old legends,' said one of them.

'She asked a question but she didn't get an answer,' said the other brother.

They laughed aloud but they soon stopped when they saw a cloud of fire-flies coming towards them and heard a moaning from the bushes…

Student Book Chapter 7

Activity 1: Real or not?

Imaginary. No. No. People being hanged for no good reason, arch being hanged, way of choosing king, coconut as king.

Activity 3: Summarising plot to draw a storyboard

King. Because or false pride (to make himself look good to the people). The arch was too low. Yes. Because people look foolish. For example, 'City of False Pride and Fools'. Boss builder, workers, some sellers, planner, arch. Should say no. Because he was a man of his word and he was the tallest. It was like having no king to worry about.

Activity 4: Themes

Possible theme: foolish pride.

Activity 8: True or imaginary

True; yes; yes; facts are given.

Activity 9: comparing an imaginary and a real story

Sample answers:

Coconut City	*The Oldest Spade*
This is an imaginary story.	This is a real story.
The characters are important in the story	The characters are not so important in the story.
There is an imaginary plot that is the actions of the characters.	There is a list of facts.
The setting is an imaginary world called Coconut City.	The setting is the real world of Papua New Guinea.
The theme is that foolish pride makes you act in a silly way.	The theme is how important it is to take care of things that are important to our culture.
The problems in the story were: who was to blame.	The problems in the story were: how to keep the spade safe.
The story ends with a resolution.	The story ends with a conclusion.

Activity 10: Questions about 'The Oldest Spade'

1. Some people digging ditches. 2. No.
3. It is the oldest spade found so far. 4. To find out how old wood is. 5. About 9000 years ago.
6. It shows how PNG was a leader in developing agriculture.

Activity 13: Is it fact or opinion?

1. F 2. O 3. F 4. O 5. O 6. F 7 F 8 F 9. F 10. F. All sentences in the factual story 'The Oldest Spade' are facts.

Activity 15: Answer these questions

1. True.
2. Information is given, imagination is not used.

3. *Opinions*: 'Lazy man, that Jacob,'; 'He hasn't done anything to make his farm.'; They said that Jacob spent all day sitting doing nothing in trees.; 'That is more important than your fences.' His neighbours said to themselves that he was still lazy and now he was silly too. The other sentences are facts.
4. Yes. Jacob and the forest itself.
5. Yes, looking after nature.
6. For example, how we should take care of forests.

Student Book Chapter 8

Activity 10: Thoughts about poems

'The Changing Times'

1. Not in the distant past. Could be any time since colonialists came. He talks about changes brought by colonialists.
2. 'My old ways of life'.
3. Traditions and customs.
4. White man's civilisation.
5. Not at first, but then he does.

'Poem' by Mary Toliman

1. Any time, but probably recent, because now there is a need to talk about keeping traditions and stories. In the past it happened naturally.
2. Oral traditional story telling, with the elders of the clan telling their children and grandchildren.
3. To keep the stories that are a history of their village.

'Refugee in Bougainville'

1. Within recent times. This is when the Bougainville crisis happened.
2. Because he feels like a stranger in his own land.
3. About losing everything and being in danger.

'Family Love' by Jilly J

1. Probably recent: lollies, church marriage.
2. Yes.
3. Yes.

'Malasang children's paddle song'

1. Traditional times, but could still be sung.
2. Drowning and sharks.
3. *The sea will be happy to get us; the waves are out of breath*

'Sepik Daughter' by Lusey Goro

1. Recent times.
2. Someone else. The writer does not agree.

'Prayer song from Oro Province'

1. Traditional times, but could still be sung.
2. Yes. Plants don't grow.
3. Garden to dry out, tapa to dry, weeds not to grow.

Student Book Chapter 10

Activity 2: Using some of the ways to learn how to spell

ear; class, ass, room; pie; clock, lock, wise; mess, sage, age.

Activity 4: Checking spelling using your dictionary

accent, cruise, ballet, conflict, drought, faeces, guard, lotion, pagan, safari, vase, court, action, thought, taught, write/right

Activity 5: Checking what kind of word it is

bag (noun), proud (adjective), bilum (noun), boot (noun), tremble (verb), corrupt (adjective/verb)

Activity 6: Checking meaning

loan; quiet; loose; passed; aloud

Activity 7: The work of words in a sentence

- The old (adjective) woman (noun) carried (verb) the heavy (adjective) bilum (noun).
- I cut (verb) the ripe (adjective) pawpaw (noun).
- We chased (verb) the naughty (adjective) dog (noun).
- Mother (noun) cooked (verb) the fresh (adjective) greens (noun).
- I dug (verb) the big (adjective) hole (noun).

Activity 8: Using the right adjective

good baby; green mango; full bottle; correct answer; brave soldier

Activity 11: Using synonyms

right; same; wrong; medium; later; start

Activity 13: Changing present tense to past tense

1. The girls beat the tapa.
2. Two boys made nets.
3. The children caught fish.

4. My cat had grey fur.
5. The book fell on the floor.
6. Yellow was my favourite colour.
7. The boys cut the grass.
8. I ate fish.
9. I washed my dog.
10. My mother sold coconuts on the side of the road.

Activity 15: Are these sentences?

Joe sat by the river. Yes.

To hear her tell the story. No.

At the weekend in the city. No.

Next week I will begin to write a story every day. Yes.

Our school has a new fence. Yes.

Learning the rules. No.

Until the weekend. No.

My dog is always hungry. Yes.

Walking along the beach. No.

Because I am tall. No.

Activity 16: Using different kinds of sentences

(Sample sentences, pupils' answers may vary. Make sure sentences have verbs and subjects.)

- Look out for the wild dog, Sally!
- Pato, come on and hurry up or we will be late.
- Is the food too hot for you?
- Storekeeper, tell me how much that shirt costs.
- Pupils, please sit.

Activity 17: Making phrases into sentences

(Sample sentences, pupils' answers may vary. Make sure sentences have verbs and subjects.)

- There was a market at the gate.
- I left my plate inside the house.
- The boy on the bike ran off the road.
- I went home from school with a headache.
- Sammy picked the mangoes for the old man.
- The children danced in the rain.

Activity 18: Adding capital letters and full stops

Sipaia left the house with her school bag. She met her friend Nenci at the path. Then they walked to school along the highway. They looked out for big trucks. They did this every morning. Today was different because there had been a big storm in the night. There was no traffic on the road. They knew that the bridge must have been washed away.

For you to try: We have a lot of whales in the ~~see~~ sea near ~~papua~~ Papua New Guinea. If ~~if~~ you ~~gone~~ go to the coast near Siassi ~~Iland~~ Island, you ~~were~~ will see whales.

In the ~~passed~~ *past* many ~~countrys~~ *countries* ~~like~~ *liked* to catch whales. The whales ~~is~~ *were* used to make oil. People also ~~eat~~ *ate* the ~~meet~~ *meat.* The bones ~~was use two~~ *were used too.* Some kinds of whales were killed ~~to~~ *too* much. This ~~meaning~~ *means* there are not ~~much~~ *many* of them left now. One kind that is ~~all most~~ *almost* gone is the Blue Whale. It is the ~~bigest~~ *biggest* animal on Earth ~~too day~~ *today.*

There is a law to stop people killing ~~whales some~~ *whales. Some* governments don't like this law. Only people who catch whales because it is their ~~traditional, food~~ *traditional food* can catch whales. If whales are not ~~look out~~ *looked after* we may not have whales in the ~~see~~ *sea* any more.

Student Book Chapter 11

Activity 5: Asking questions about how stories work

1. Yes. It tells that the story is about one day in someone's life. On that day there was a gumi race.
2. Who, what, when, why?
3. Yes, yes
4. The sister was saved, and knew the writer wasn't scared.

Student Book Chapter 12

Activity 6: Using strong verbs

1. peered; gazed; stared; glanced
2. limped; marched; strode; strutted; strolled
3. announced; apologised; warned; suggested; admitted

Activity 7: making a poem stronger

Verse 2: dawdles on fly out splashing shooting striving to ceases

Verse 3: speed tittering struggling to heed swirls on stroll

Appendix 7: Glossary

Student Book Chapter 1

speaking in different ways we use our voice differently for different circumstances (in different places, for different purposes and when speaking to different people).

role play a role play is like a small drama written by the students and performed for the class. Students are asked to step outside their normal personalities and 'become' another person, thinking about how that person would speak and act.

poetry poetry helps the reader think about familiar things in different ways. It uses language, rhythm, rhyme and structure to capture the essence of a feeling, thought, object or scene.

important in the community this concept is part of the syllabus. It means to speak and listen, read and write about issues, ideas or problems which matter to the community of which your school and students are part.

read aloud students need to say words clearly in a voice which can be heard, pronouncing words correctly. Begin with reading in pairs, then to a few more, then to a larger group and finally aloud to the class.

story telling using voice to make a story interesting by expressing emotions. Listening skills: to sustain listening for a period of time.

advertisements information that can be seen or heard which is aimed at making the reader or listener buy something.

re-write to take the original piece of writing and make changes to it.

Student Book Chapter 2

question words these are words which begin a question. Your listeners know that a question will follow when they hear these words.

information facts and ideas about a topic.

survey a group of questions about a topic to find out information or opinions about a topic. A survey has a particular purpose which is the reason why the questions are asked.

polite this is an adjective to describe treating some-one with respect and using good manners.

reporting when you find out information you then pass the information on to someone else. This is called reporting. A 'report' is what you write or speak.

gestures these are movements we make with our bodies. They add to the words we speak with our mouths and help our listeners understand.

conduct *(verb)* this means carry out or do—so 'conduct your own survey' means do your own survey.

Student Book Chapter 3

sense to make sense means to have a meaning that can be understood.

conversation speaking and listening between two or more people.

instructions a list of things about how to do something, given in a certain order.

directions these are like instructions but they tell you how to get from one place to another place.

signal this is a name for words that tell your listener what is coming next when you are giving instructions or directions.

order the way in which things are arranged, one thing following another.

formal we use formal speech when we want to show respect, or when we do not know the person we are speaking to.

Student Book Chapter 4

context where events, for example, a conversation, are taking place, who is there and what reason they are there for.

purpose the reason for speaking or writing.

audience who you are speaking to or writing for.

bias favouring one side over another.

stereotype giving the same characteristics to everybody without changing your ideas to suit individuals.

findings what you find out from asking questions. Findings are an important part of a report.

Student Book Chapter 5

real world factual stories about real events, places and characters.

imaginary world stories which come from the imagination of the writer. They will often have a basis in factual events, places and characters.

events the series of actions which make up the plot.

characters both factual and imaginative stories can have characters. However, character is usually more important in an imaginative story. Characters perform the actions which make up the plot of the story. Character is important in biography (factual).

title the name of the story which should give some clue to the content of the story.

information facts such as names, dates, statistics, observable habits.

orientation to orient someone is to give them important information they need to interpret something such as a story. Orientation provides that important information at the beginning to help guide the reader.

complication this is part of the plot that makes the story interesting. There can be conflict.

resolution if there has been conflict or a problem in the story, the author will offer a solution or conclusion which is the resolution.

time words/signals these are clues the author uses to help the reader follow the sequence of events in a story.

narrative a narrative tells a realistic or imagined story. It is written to entertain, stimulate, motivate, guide and teach the reader. Examples include myths, legends, fables, fairy tales, short stories and picture books.

sequence a series of events that happen in order.

chronological sequence the series of events follow the sequence of real time.

cartoons stories with pictures. The characters in the stories have speech bubbles showing what they are saying. A cartoon can be short—three of four separate pictures, or it can be as long as a book.

cartoon balloons/bubbles the speech or thought of the character(s) in the cartoon is shown in an enclosed bubble or balloon coming from the mouth of the character.

shadow puppet The puppet is an outline only.

process the way in which something is made or done.

Student Book Chapter 6

punctuation a system of marks used to break writing into manageable parts. The most common punctuation marks are the full stop, question mark, comma, apostrophe and quotation mark. They tell the reader when to slow down or stop and make meaning clear.

word attack skills a series of skills the students need in order to understand the meaning of a pronunciation of words they have not previously encountered.

context (for word attack skills) the other words in the sentence, and the general meaning of a sentence or passage in which the new words are found which provide clues as to the meaning, pronunciation of the unknown word.

rhythm all speech has rhythm. In ordinary speech we stress some syllables and not others. In poetry this stress is taken further and is used by the poet to make a pattern of strong and weak sounds.

pattern this is repetition of a series of things. In sound it can be the repetition of a certain number of sounds in a line.

repeated done over again. Sounds can be repeated, ideas can be repeated, words can be repeated. It is one of the ways a poet uses to draw the reader's attention to the meaning of a poem.

sound unit/syllable words are broken into sound units. This has nothing to do with the length of the word, but how many different sounds the reader needs to say in a word.

verse a 'paragraph' in a poem.

key word an important word that carries meaning in a sentence.

phrase group of words in a sentence. A phrase is not usually used on its own, except where the context makes meaning clear. Examples of phrases; under the tree, running quickly, over the road.

summary a shortened version of a longer passage in which the essential information is kept and non-essential information is left out.

heading the title of a passage. In some writing such as reports, there are main headings and sub-headings. The heading should help the reader guess/predict what is to follow.

topic sentence the most important sentence in a paragraph. The topic sentence gives the main idea that is developed in a paragraph.

headline the heading of a newspaper report or article.

predicting making a guess about the content of a passage by taking words in a heading or headline and relating them to your own knowledge and experience.

Student Book Chapter 7

plot what happens in a story, storyline, events, actions.

theme a message that the author wants the reader

	to understand. Themes are often not stated by the author, but the reader needs to look out for them as they help understanding of the story.
setting	where (place setting) and when (time setting) the story happens. In some stories the setting can be a very important part of the reader's understanding.
ending	the final part of a story, conclusion, resolution of a conflict.
fact/factual	based on things that are known to be true, they can be seen or proved.
opinion	what someone thinks about facts.
action	events in a story, rather than passages of description.
conflict	two different sets of ideas or ways of acting meet.
compare	to take two or more events, places, people etc. and show how they are similar and what differences they have (contrasts).

Student Book Chapter 8

genre	the different types of writing that have their own features. Texts are arranged to suit their purpose and readers can observe these different structures. Some examples are: instructions, arguments, narrative.
personal preference	an individual's feeling towards actions, events, people etc.
dilemma	a difficult choice.
alternatives	different ways in which a problem can be solved or an action etc. done.
justify	to give reason why a certain view should be held or choice made.

Student Book Chapter 9

writing process	process and product are two parts of the same concept. The process is the steps that are taken over time to reach the product.
free writing	this is a kind of brainstorming. The students should not be restricted by spelling rules, or controlled as to content (within reason).
plan	an outline of action to be taken.
draft	a preliminary writing, not meant to be the final copy.
edit	to think about and weigh up the content as to logic, sufficiency, excess, order of presentation etc. and to apply rules of spelling and grammar.
habit	something that you do without thinking, because you have done it so often.
routine	a regular way of doing things.
usually	normally happening, expected.
tips	suggestions to help.
letter	communication in writing addressed to another person.

Student Book Chapter 10

strategies	ways of approaching a problem to solve it.
work of words	each word in a sentence has a role which gives meaning to the sentence.
adjective	a word which provides additional information about a noun.
synonym	a word with a similar meaning.
verb	the word which tells the action happening in a sentence, what the subject of the sentence does.
tense	verbs have forms which indicate to the reader the tense or what time the action is happening.
capital letter	upper case letter.
full stop	(.) dot that indicates the end of a sentence.
exclamation mark	(!) mark used to express surprise, delight, pain or shock.
question mark	(?) mark used to tell the reader that the sentence is a question.
comma	(,) mark used to indicate a pause, or to clarify meaning.
speech mark	(") marks used to enclose dialogue.

Student Book Chapter 11

journal	a personal writing method.
autobiography	a true life story, written by the person the story is about.
personal letter	a letter to a person you know, about personal matters, such as family.
business letter	a letter written about business matters, in recognised formal style and format.
essay	a short piece of writing about a particular subject, following the conventions for essay writing—introduction, body, conclusion.

Student Book Chapter 12

weak and strong words	weak words do not give the reader a complete picture. Strong words tell the reader more clearly what the writer means and add to understanding.
personal preference	what you as a person like, not necessarily based on facts.